WADSWORTH PHILC

CW01468346

# ON

# PLOTINUS

**C. Wayne Mayhall**
*University of Wales*

THOMSON

—✳—™

WADSWORTH

Australia • Canada • Mexico • Singapore • Spain • United Kingdom • United States

Printed in Canada
1  2  3  4  5  6  7 07  06  05  04  03

Printer: Transcontinental-Louiseville

ISBN: 0-534-25229-X

**For more information about our products, contact us at:**
**Thomson Learning Academic**
**Resource Center**
**1-800-423-0563**

**For permission to use material from this text, contact us by:**
**Phone: 1-800-730-2214**
**Fax: 1-800-731-2215**
**Web: www.thomsonrights.com**

For more information contact:
**Wadsworth-Thomson Learning**
**10 Davis Drive**
**Belmont, CA 94002-3098**
**USA**

**Asia**
Thomson Learning
5 Shenton Way #01-01
UIC Building
Singapore 068808

**Australia/New Zealand**
Thomson Learning
102 Dodds Street
Southbank, Victoria 3006
Australia

**Canada**
Nelson
1120 Birchmount Road
Toronto, Ontario M1K 5G4
Canada

**Europe/Middle East/South Africa**
Thomson Learning
High Holborn House
50-51 Bedford Row
London WC1R 4LR
United Kingdom

**Latin America**
Thomson Learning
Seneca, 53
Colonia Polanco
11560 Mexico D.F.
Mexico

**Spain/Portugal**
Paraninfo Thomson Learning
Calle/Magallanes, 25
28015 Madrid, Spain

# For Christian Journey Fontenot

*We have not been cut away; we are not separate, what though the body-nature has closed about us to press us to itself; we breathe and hold our ground because the Supreme does not give and pass but gives on for ever, so long as it remains what it is.*

---Plotinus (*Sixth Ennead, Tractate 9, Treatise 9*)

# Contents

# Preface

Nearly two millennia ago, in his *Tractate* on *Our Tutelary Spirit*, the mystical philosopher Plotinus delivered a poignant declaration of mind over matter. He wrote:

> This is why we must break away towards the High: we dare not keep ourselves set towards the sensuous principle, following the images of the sense, or towards the merely vegetative, intent upon the gratifications of eating and procreation; our life must be pointed towards...God (III – 4:2).

"The Plotinian theme par excellence," writes Plotinian scholar, Emile Brehier, in his *Philosophy of Plotinus*, "is that of the solitude of the sage who is alone with the supreme principle which he has attained because he has successively abandoned all...reality (POP, 7)."

There are no friends, family, or fellow citizens in this solitary country for it is the counterpart of a different world "peopled by benevolent or malevolent beings, into which the mythologies and religions usher the soul after death," Brehier reminds us.

As Hamlet spoke to Horatio, "There are more things in heaven and earth than are dreamt of in your philosophy," and Brehier rightly notes that the modern belief of a sensible world which holds an infinite set of new problems the mind must overcome in order to understand, has created the need for reason to rise above the senses in order to comprehend them.

Perhaps such a transcendental flight awaits the reader who takes up a copy of Stephen MacKenna's translation of *The Enneads* in one hand and this brief introduction *On Plotinus* in the other. The act itself, as MacKenna would say, is its own reward of "perfect clearness and expressive cadence."

I would like to thank Dan Kolak, *Wadsworth Philosophers Series* editor, for helpful comments and for the opportunity to spend time with Plotinus, the founder of neo-Platonism and one of philosophy's most important influences in late classical, medieval, Christian, Islamic and Renaissance thought.

Citations frequently referenced are: LOP – *Porphyry: On the Life of Plotinus*, appears in *The Enneads of Plotinus*, Penguin Classics edition; EP – *The Essential Plotinus*; PN – *Plotinus and Neoplatonism*; POP – *Philosophy of Plotinus*. Citations with the format (IV – 1:2) refer to *The Enneads of Plotinus*, Penguin Classics edition.

# 1
# Introduction

*...in Plotinus the fusion of religion, ethics, and metaphysics is almost complete. He must be studied as a spiritual director, a prophet and not only a thinker. His is one of the most ambitious of all philosophical systems, for he not only attempts to unite and reconcile what was best in all Greek philosophy, but he claims to have found the way of deliverance and salvation for the soul of man, in whatever circumstances he may be placed* (POP, 7).

## Neo-Platonism

Platonism as a philosophical movement generally refers to the study of the philosophy of Plato and/or the philosophy of any movement after Plato's time which bases its approach on Platonian themes and absorbs virtually every nonmaterialist and religious doctrine of systems prior to it.

Plotinus (205-70) is one of the founding fathers of the Platonist movement referred to as *neo-Platonism*. He and two other notable thinkers, Iamblichus (245-326) and Proclus (412-85), considered themselves to be disciples of Plato (427-347 BC), although they often disagreed with much of his thought.

Historians have divided the neo-Platonic tradition into three main periods. Plotinus and his immediate followers are the third century school known as the "Plotinian" School. Iamblichus and his followers, known as the "Syrian" School, are the fourth century disciples. The fifth century followers, known as the "Athenian" School, were led by Plutarch of Athens and included Proclus, its most prolific philosopher, Syrianus, and their successors.

Each period had its own distinct and innovative appropriation of Platonic thought but certain themes are common to all three. For the neo-Platonist, as for Plato, ultimate reality is the One, which is identified with God as the highest being and with the Good as its very character and nature. Emanating or coming forth from the One are the 'hypostases' or substances which comprise metaphysical reality: One; Mind; Soul.

Matter or evil are not independent entities apart from these hypostases and in fact are not even to be considered as real. All things are derived from the One, the highest principle, resemble and imitate it, and eventually return to it, so that the movement of all things are away from the unity of the One toward disunity and back toward the One and to unity.

In its simplest description, the neo-Platonist's purpose was to develop and disseminate a personal understanding of theology and metaphysics, begun by the great Athenian philosopher Plato almost a century before, which would result in an understanding of higher reality.

## Plotinus' Beginnings

Plotinus was born in Lykopolis, Upper Egypt around 205 A.D. and died of a disease (possibly tuberculosis or leprosy) in Minturno, Rome, around 270. He was 28-years-old when he began to study philosophy in Alexandria, Egypt (history records him as having been a Hellenized Egyptian rather than a Greek native). His first teachers were not able to satisfy his thirst for knowledge, however, so he sought out a more worthy mentor.

It was the teaching of Ammonius Sakkas which made a lasting impression on Plotinus and the young philosopher sat under his tutelage for almost eleven years before embarking on an expedition with the army of Emperor Gordianus III. Sakkas' history with Plotinus is sketchy but recent scholarship has discovered the impact the great teacher had on his student by comparing the doctrines of Plotinus with those of the Christian theologian and biblical scholar, Origen, who was also a student of Sakkas.

Plotinus' service with Gordianus' army was short-lived. In 244, the Emperor was slain by his own soldiers in a battle against Persia. Forced to flee for his life, Plotinus made for Rome (by way of Antioch, Greece) and arrived there that same year.

## Plotinus' Circle

At some point after his arrival in Rome Plotinus began to teach at a school of philosophy he was able to establish on land granted to him by the emperor Gallienus, who might have saw in Plotinus a potential ally in his campaign to revive paganism throughout the empire. After teaching in the school for nearly a decade and forming a sort of neo-Platonian community of pupils devoted to living by the rule of Plato, Plotinus began to take his writing more seriously and to organize his teaching for this purpose.

Philosophical discussion was at the heart of Plotinus' Circle and pupils came from around the vast Roman Empire to join in. Amelius, a dedicated pupil, gave his fellow pupil and eventual Plotinian biographer, Porphyry, an account of the earlier years of teaching in Rome:

> The sessions, Amelius told me, were confused and much nonsense was spoken since he [Plotinus] stimulated enquiry among the participants (LOP, 3).

In 263, when Porphyry joined the Circle he was careful to record what he discovered. A pupil would begin the meeting by reading from a commentary on Plato or Aristotle, for example, and Plotinus would immediately offer his own self-styled commentary on what had just been read, careful to avoid a passage-for-passage exegesis, but instead opting for a sort of editorial monologue on it, followed by an open discussion of this collision of thoughts.

Debate naturally ensued and quite often utter chaos erupted in an admixture of shouting between several of those from opposing camps and quiet conversation among a few who agreed, while Plotinus, all the while, would not attempt to impose himself among the fray. Porphyry writes that "his teaching seemed like a conversation and he did not reveal immediately to anyone the logical necessities contained in what he said (LOP, 18)."

Porphyry gives an example of another debate when Plotinus left him somewhat confused and aggravated:

> For three days I, Porphyry, asked him how soul is with the body and he persisted in his explanation. A certain Thaumasius came in and said that he wanted to hear an overall treatment to be put in books and that he could not bear Prophyry's answers and questions. But Plotinus said, 'But if we do not solve the difficulties raised by Porphyry's questions, we will not be able to say anything to be put in a book (LOP, 18).'

In this chapter Porphyry brings us very near to Plotinus the man:

> When he spoke his intellect illuminated even his face. Of pleasing aspect, he was then even more beautiful to see. Sweating slightly, his gentleness showed as did his kindness while being questioned and his rigour (LOP, 18).

Gallienus was murdered in 268 and two years later Plotinus died. Somewhere between these two years Plotinus' Circle crumbled, perhaps partially because of its political connections, but more likely because in 269 Porphyry became ill with serious depression and under his master's advice left for Sicily. Plotinus, already quite ill himself, could no longer hold his community together.

## Porphyry

Plotinus' works were all written in the sixteen years after 253 and it is Porphyry who recorded them for posterity. Plotinus' sketchy biography, Porphyry's *Life of Plotinus*, is an ancient classic and unarguably one of the most interesting ancient biographies to survive history. Both the *Life of Plotinus* and his works (*The Enneads*) were included in one edition by Porphyry, published approximately thirty years after Plotinus' death.

Porphyry arranged Plotinus' works into six sections called "enneads" (Greek for "nine") because each contains nine treatises. He arbitrarily created some treatises by dissecting or combining the originals, although each section (with the exception of the *Sixth Ennead*) has a common focus. Independent of this arrangement, he indicated when each treatise was written by assigning it to one of three periods in the life of Plotinus:

1. 253-263, before he became Plotinus' student
2. 263-268, while he was his student
3. 268-270, after he left for Sicily

This monograph will follow, quite loosely, these three periods of Porphyry. The standard citation to Plotinus' work designates: the number of the ennead first, by Roman numeral; the treatise second, by Arabic numeral; and the place of the treatise in Porphyry's chronological enumeration third.

# Influences

Plotinus did not create his philosophy inside a vacuum. Many and diverse were the schools of thought from which he draws insight into the mysteries of the universe. Concerning Plotinus' three hypostasis (substances) - the One, the *Nous*, and the Soul - a pre-history leading up to Plotinus' work is helpful and a portion of each chapter in which this tripartite division of reality is considered will be devoted to such a Prelude. At present the influence of Plato and Aristotle, the Pythagoreans and Stoics will be considered.

## *Plato*

*Parmenides*, *The Sophist*, *Timeus*, and *The Second Letter* are four of Plato's writings which seem to best explain an overall view of his metaphysics. Each of these are short works and can be easily digested prior to a study of *The Enneads*. As a result Plotinus' positioning of ideas will make more sense.

For Plato all reality is encompassed in two realms, the realm of *Ideas* or *Intelligibles* and the realm of *Sensibles*. Only Intelligibles are the inner essential nature of a thing or its true being, what the Greeks knew as *ousia*, or essence. Intelligibles, then, must be both eternal and changeless.

Take for example the Idea of the Good. Plato placed the Good above all other things, even beyond "being" itself. Like the sun, which Plato uses as an example throughout his writings, the Good is the source of all being for all existing things. History holds no secret regarding Plato's identification of the Good with his Idea of the One, or the Supreme Creator of heaven and earth.

In *Parmenides*, Plato expands on his idea of the One but does not draw his explanation to a close. He reaches the conclusion of the majority of his contemporaries that the One, ultimately, remains a mystery and is unknowable:

> And if there be anything that has absolute knowledge, there is nothing more likely than God to have this most exact knowledge?
> Certainly.
> But then, will God, having this absolute knowledge, have a knowledge of human things?

And why not?

Because the ideas have no relation to human notions, nor human notions to them; the relations of either are in their respective spheres (EP, 1165).

In his dialogue, *The Sophist*, Plato contradicts his thoughts above by embracing the idea of mutability (change) and knowledge (how could the One think without a mind) to his realm of Ideas. The conversation is between a stranger and the philosopher Theaetetus. He writes:

> *Stranger*: And what about the assertors of the all and one – must we not endeavor to ascertain from them what they mean by "being?"
> *Theaetetus*: By all means.
> *S*: Then let us ask a question of them: "One, you say, alone is?"
> "Yes," they will reply.
> *T*: True
> *S*: And , again, being is?
> *T*: Yes.
> *S*: And is being the same as one, and do you apply two names to the same thing?
> *T*: What will be their answer to that, Stranger?
> *S*: It is clear, Theaetetus, that he who asserts the unity of being will find a difficulty in answering this or any other question.
> *T*: How is that?
> *S*: To admit of two names, and to affirm that there is nothing but unity, is surely ridiculous?
> *T*: Certainly.

Regarding the sense world, in his *Timaeus* Plato presents the beginnings of the universe in mythological fashion, presenting the Demiurge (a divine but not omnipotent architect) as the potter who takes the clay (Plato's "receptacle") of existence and creates from out of nothing (although he looks to the Forms for ideas), similar to the *creatio ex nihilo* (Latin: creation out of/from nothing) of the God of Judeo-Christian theology.

This *nihilo* of Plato contains no qualities but instead, Plato doesn't explain how, ideas as Forms have infiltrated the void (or were always just there) and remain as images or shapes and structures, abstractions of the created world. These Forms are eternal, changeless, and incorporeal (immaterial, matterless) and we can have knowledge of them only through thought.

The Demiurge creates a cosmic soul in addition to the known universe and imparts immortality to each individual soul as well as a geometrical configuration which unites both the cosmic and individual souls in unity. Plato writes:

> And this is most true; for the divine power suspended the head and root of us from that place where the generation of the soul first began, and thus made erect the whole body (EP, 1216-17).

A doctrine of reincarnation applies to all individual souls, according to Plato, and the essence of these souls implies that they necessarily are both eternal and immortal.

In the *Second Letter* Plato writes of three realms: the first related to "the king," or the Demiurge; the second to the second, or the Forms; the third to the third, or the *Intelligibles* and *Sensibles*. Plotinus believes these three realms Plato refers to are in fact the One, the *Nous*, and the Soul.

## *Aristotle*

Aristotle has been characterized as either an anti-Platonist from the very beginning of his encounter with Plato's Academy as a teenager or as having slowly moved away from Plato's philosophy over time. Whichever the case might have been, Plato's realm where a Demiurge mediates between Ideas and Sensibles was untenable for him. In place of the ideal Forms, Aristotle searched for a more pragmatic, scientific basis for reality which did not posit invisible and ineffable entities as possible origins.

Aristotle's solution comes in the form of theory of substance (ousia), where the "primary substance" or ultimate reality consists of concrete things, without whose existence nothing else would exist. Plotinus' levels of reality, or as it will be considered in this work, his tripartite composition of reality, appears to be a synthesis of Aristotelian and Platonian metaphysics.

Aristotle's Intelligence (*Nous*) is also appropriated by Plotinus. According to Aristotle, the Intelligence alone is immortal and is superior to the rest of the soul, which is only just the "form" of the body and does not possess Intelligence. Supreme deity, for him, is Intelligence contemplating itself.

## *Pythagoreanism and Stoicism*

The writings of Philolaus, a Pythagorean, influenced Aristotle and Plato (see *Philebus*), and, ultimately, Plotinus. Philolaus argued that the cosmos and its contents were composed of limiters (shapes which are the structure) and *unlimiteds* (material elements such as earth, air, fire and water which are structured). True reality for Philolaus is the admixture of limiters and unlimiteds bound together in a harmony that can be expressed mathematically.

Another influence was the strictly materialistic (matter alone exists) and immanentistic (being within, or inside, as opposed to *transcendent*) Stoic doctrine of the omnipresence of the divine in the cosmos. A *logos* (also "reason," "God," "nature," "fate") forms the universe which is composed of matter. The human mind is a 'seed' of the logos, and the purpose of an individual life is to come to understand the logos and its purposes.

## Plotinus and Platonism

The decline of Stoicism in the later second century and the increasingly other-worldly religiosity of the period left the intellectual arena clear for Platonism, and in particular for the neo-Platonic school, the last of the great philosophical schools of antiquity, founded by Plotinus. The philosophy of Plotinus is, nevertheless, overwhelmingly Platonic in inspiration as we have already explored briefly in the introduction.

A few qualifications regarding the Platonic influence upon the work of Plotinus are necessary. First of all, although inspired by Plato, the neo-Platonic tradition is not concerned with historical details, with the circumstances under which Plato wrote and the contemporary problems he dealt with. It is the body of timeless truths and their immediate reflection on metaphysical reality which primarily concerns Plotinus and his followers.

Secondly, Platonism has looked for a static body of dogma (where it has not been content with inspiration of a poetic character), and thus it has tended to minimize the tentative and less systematic aspects of Plato's philosophizing.

The essence of Platonism is its exhibition of the very type of a metaphysical philosophy particularly directed toward a transcendent reality. With this goes the rationalistic side of the Platonic tradition, a belief in the power of thought directly to grasp transcendent realities, as shown in Platonic theories of universals and of mathematical objects; thus logic and mathematics are seen as providing keys to the structure of the universe.

A further correlate is the belief in degrees of reality, and another is the Platonic doctrine of the immortality of the soul: Platonism is strongly opposed to anything that can be called materialism. Plotinus' work, then, is more dogmatic and less tentative than Plato. It is concerned with constructing a system for which Plato's dialogues could provide "proof-texts." Much that is central is not, in its Plotinian form, to be found in Plato at all.

The reader who encounters *The Enneads* for the first time will soon discover why it is often said of Plotinus' work that it doesn't fit easily into either ancient or medieval philosophy and that his writing is often obtuse and meandering.

To truly appreciate the work of Plotinus an overwhelming amount of background (historical and philosophical) is necessary and because his writings are not well-preserved by his pupils this background information is not always easy to come by.

This lack of background coupled with Plotinus' somewhat random order of presenting his philosophy in *The Enneads* can leave the reader searching for a definitive statement on any particular subject in a particular section of the work. In short, to put together Plotinus' comprehensive view regarding a certain philosophical position in *The Enneads* can prove to be a daunting task. This introduction, however, through a categorical presentation of the overarching Plotinian' themes intends to make this process a little less frustrating.

The main conception is that of the three divine hypostases, or natures, which are, in descending order, the One, the *Nous*, and the Soul. It is to a closer examination of these three hypostases we now turn.

# 2

# The One

*We do not, it is true, grasp it by knowledge, but that does not mean that we are utterly void of it ... unable to state it, we may still possess it ... above reason, mind and feeling; conferring these powers, not to be confounded with them...A single, unmanifold emanation we may very well allow - how even that can come from a pure unity may be a problem, but we may always explain it on analogy of the irradiation from a luminary - but a multitudinous production raises questions* (V – 3:14-15).

## The Plotinian "One"

Into the rather confusing world of the Stoics and Skeptics, Plotinus emerges as the quintessential neo-Platonist, convinced an amalgamation of the great sage's ideas and his own are needed in confusing times to confront a growing range of philosophical quandaries. He asks a familiar question once again. What is this "it" that we cannot grasp by knowledge or talk about but are able to possess?

For Plotinus, to develop a comprehensive theory of the One, or the First, as the highest principle or cause is necessary because there must be a principle of everything that is. The One, therefore, is omnipresent but is itself above being. It is absolutely transcendental.

Since it is above being, it is fully indetermined (qualityless), although it may be called the Good as the object of universal desire. Because it is one, it is entirely undifferentiated (without multiplicity). As every act of cognition, even of self-cognition, presupposes the duality of object and subject, Plotinus repeatedly and strongly states that the One is void of any cognition and is ignorant even of itself.

He tries to mitigate this statement in some places, hesitatingly attributing to the One some kind of self- or quasi-awareness, of its "power" to engender being. In other places he distinguishes the ordinary kind of ignorance from the ignorance of the One and says that there is nothing of which the One is cognizant but that there is also nothing of which it is ignorant.

In this chapter further explanation of Plotinus' often illusive characterization of the One will be explored, including the idea of the One in light of the Many, the One and space, the One and being, thought, and purpose, and the One as unthinkable. Before we proceed, however, a very brief history of the idea of a "Supreme Being" such as "God," or in Plotinus' case "the One," is in order.

## A Prelude to the Plotinian One

What is behind or beyond the universe, if anything? And if there is some "thing", to use the word quite loosely, what is its character and nature? Is it person or a field of force familiar to the quantum physicist? If the former, how does it communicate with mankind, or does it? Can we even begin to comprehend the reality of its existence?

Historically, a little less than 5,000 years ago, the Hebrew culture embraced and, quite often, rebelled against the existence of one true God and the true reality of only one god among the pluralism of the age. His name was YHWH (Yahweh), spelled out in the original Hebrew language using only consonants as a symbol of reverence to Him, maker of heaven and earth and sovereign ruler of all creatures great and small. Long before Jewish culture revered and worshiped YHWH, however, there were many gods responsible for the creation and upkeep of the created universe - a god of the sky, a god of fire, a goddess of wisdom and a god of the sun, for examples.

Like the Hebrew culture before them, the Stoics (circa 300 BC) believed the universe was formed and guided by a *logos*, or reason, (except this self was composed of matter) and this fundamental substance could be referred to as one God, related to the world just as the soul is related to the human body. A skeptic of Stoicism, Carneades (214-129 BC) denied that the human reason can approach a true knowledge of God. He believed the idea that the human mind might comprehend the very existence of God is itself patently absurd.

### Greek gods

Zeus sat on the throne of the pantheon of Greek mythological figures with his wife Hera by his side. He was not unaccustomed to the ways of mortal man yet there was no room to doubt his reign was without rival.

But there were other theories vying for validity in the Greek world view, too. Thales (640-546 BC), for example, tried to explain the world's existence and all other things in natural ways and without injecting the idea of divine beings into the metaphysic. Anaximander (610-546 BC), on the other hand, believed the original substance from which everything originated was "the infinite," but he did not associate his ideas with those of the gods. Xenophanes (570-480), more closely related to Platonic thought perhaps, taught that God is the universe's most fundamental principle, that he is the world and the whole of living nature. This belief that everything in the universe is God, and God is everything in the universe is known as pantheism. For Xenophanes, God is the "One and All" and there is only one God, and this God is the universe.

## Plato and Aristotle

In the introduction a brief idea of the thinking of Plato and Aristotle regarding the idea of a universal absolute entity was discussed. Because of the great influence of both of these thinkers on the writings of Plotinus, clarification will be helpful.

Plato once said that "we ought to fly away from the earth as quickly as we can, and to fly away is to become like God." Man's spirit, he taught, was the stuff of heaven and the flesh and bone of the physical body were bound to the earth to which they eventually return.

For Plato, however, the word "God" had wide-ranging semantic properties. Often he is thinking of the gods just as the masses think of them, as beings governing different areas of the universe. At other times he seems to teach the existence of one supreme God who is master and ruler of the entire universe. In the *Timaeus*, he accounts for the creation of the universe by using a Demiurge, or sort of architect, who takes already-created ideas and matter and moulds the universe. In another place he speaks of the Creator as the source of souls.

The question remains; is there a plurality of gods in Plato's thought?

Aristotle is much clearer on this point than is that of Plato. Aristotle believed that there were two causes in the universe – form and matter. Forms are forces which realize themselves in the world of matter just as the idea of the artist realizes itself in marble. Hence the form is the cause of motion. Matter moves because of form. Behind form there is pure form, form without matter, and he calls this an eternal "unmoved mover," the ultimate cause of all motion, and all becoming in the universe.

This "God" is the cause of motion, but does not move himself. All the universe, every object and being in it, desires to realize itself because of God. His existence is the ultimate cause of their striving. For Aristotle God is the unifying principle and all categories of existence - things or concepts (reason) - find origin in him.

## The One as Absolute Simplex

*"The ultimate reality must be an absolute simplex (III – 8:9)."*

We can identify Plotinus' use of the word "simplex" with our more modern philosophical terminology using the Latin word "simpliciter," for they both imply an "it," if we stay with our introductory quote, which is simply, absolutely, without qualifications. The One is not subject in any way to differentiation, classification, or analysis. The one is simpliciter and not compositum – made up of distinct components.

If this is true, however, we immediately encounter what appears an insurmountable problem. How can the One serve as the source of multiplicity? How did Plotinus approach this problem? He explains:

> What comes from the Supreme cannot be identical with it and assuredly cannot be better than it - what could be better than the One and the utterly Transcendent? The emanation, then, must be less good, that is to say, less self-sufficing; now what must that be which is less self-sufficing than the One? Obviously the Not-One, that is to say, multiplicity. But multiplicity striving towards unity; that is to say, a One-that-is-Many (V – 3:14-15).

There has to be a connection, a bond between this Not-One and the One. Plotinus believes he can build a conceptual bridge between the Absolute and the particular which can connect the idea of the One with that of the multiplicity of the universe. He is not reluctant to define the One and to ask the hard questions its existence creates:

All that is not one is conserved by virtue of the One, and from One derives its characteristic nature: if it had not attained such unity as is consistent with being made up of multiplicity we could not affirm its existence: if we are able to affirm the nature of single things, this is in virtue of the unity, the identity even, which each of them possesses (V – 3:14-15).

The all-transcendent, according to Plotinus, is utterly void of multiplicity and "has no mere unity of participation but is unity's self..." He asks the question "what then is the All?" His answer is simply, "the total of which the Transcendent is the Source." How is this so? Because the Transcendent would contain only the potentiality of the universe to come.

## The One and the Many

A preliminary conclusion is that there cannot be a One which is not also a many. Plotinian scholars have argued for centuries whether or not the three aspects of the One, the *Nous*, and the Soul, are to be considered as three distinct entities or levels of being without forming some sort of unity or whether they should be considered as a Godhead or Trinity (three-as-one), to use terminology of the Christian tradition.

As used in theology, Godhead means the Supreme Being of the universe, especially comprehending all of His attributes. Godhead, too, encompasses an understanding of this Supreme Being as Trinity. Trinity, in theological terms, expresses the unity of three Persons in the one God.

The Christian doctrine is that there is only one God, one divine nature and being and this one divine Being is tri-personal, involving the distinctions of the Father, the Son, and the Holy Spirit. These three, according to doctrine, are joint partakers of the same nature and majesty of God, but are not each gods separate from one another (this would be polytheism) but one God, instead with three distinct hypostasis. The original formula in the Christian creeds is *mia ousia tres hypostaseis* (one substance, three persons).

Unlike the overtly philosophical exploration of the origins of existence and meaning Plotinus pursues in his neo-Platonic writings, the Christian faith for the better part of its history has not grounded itself in philosophical speculation but has extended the understanding of Trinitarian doctrine beyond the realm of discursive reasoning (covering a wide field of subjects), attributing knowledge of the Godhead to revelation to be accepted by faith (acceptance of things one cannot see or understand but, nonetheless, believe to be real), not to be comprehended in its depth and fullness.

Today, however, a revival in Trinitarian studies has attracted the attention of philosophers and theologians of many different backgrounds, ranging from humanistic and atheistic world-views to the many various views of world religions. For this reason, there is a revival in the ancient traditions of thought, including that of Plotinus.

## Plotinus' Godhead

Like the Father, the Son, and the Holy Spirit of Christian tradition it can be argued that the Godhead of Plotinus consists of the One, the *Nous* and the Soul, or the One-in-Many. The One in and of itself is not the Godhead but instead is the transcendent aspect of that Godhead. Plotinus says:

> The item could not make itself manifest as a One-and-all. Only the Transcendent can be that. It is the great beginning, while its sequent is a total. The Transcendent would contain the potentiality of the universe to come (V – 3:14-15).

Plotinus' understanding of these hypostases, I suggest, is certainly compatible with the thinking of other theologians and philosophers around or soon after his time, and it would not be a stretch to argue for a Trinitarian reading of *The Enneads* as this introduction does.

Consider that the Eternal contains the temporal within itself and is immanent in the temporal plane such that its presence is manifest and sustains space and time. In this sense, we are not able to take some particular characteristic of the One, such as power (omnipotence) and call this aspect the One itself.

The One is not power in the sense that a tractor has power or a body builder has the brute strength to lift a car with his teeth kind of power. Nonetheless, power comes from, or emanates from the One and has its source in the One. If the One is the Godhead, the immanence of the temporal in the eternal would be impossible. But God is not only the One. He is also the intellectual Principle and the Soul. He is One-in-Many.

15

Ultimate Reality in our universe is a One and a One-in-Many. One, because in that Ultimate Reality, the multiversal universe finds its essential unity. Many, because the universe is included, potentially, in it.

Why is it the One? Because it is the unifying principle of the multiplicity in the universe. It is an attribute, an aspect, of the Ultimate Reality, the One-in-many.

## The One and Space

Must we conclude that the One is also immanent, as He is transcendent? Plotinus insists, on the one hand, that the One is only transcendent, far removed from human qualities in its lonely majesty.

The One, in its character as the One, is transcendent, but the Neoplatonic Godhead, which includes the One, the *Nous* and the Soul or the Principle of Life, is immanent and transcendent. No Godhead can be anything else, and the arguments of the deist or the pantheist are in fact no more than a series of contradictions. The transcendent deity of the deist would not have cared to create, the immanent god of pantheism would have been powerless to do so.

It is interesting to see what Plotinus tells us of that transcendent being in its relation to the world and to space. The most important passage is as follows:

> The Principle before all these principles is no doubt the first principle of the universe, but not as immanent: immanence is not for primal sources but for engendering secondaries; that which stands as primal source of everything is not a thing but is distinct from au things; it is not, then, a member of the total but earlier than all, earlier, thus, than the Intellectual-Principle - which in fact envelops the entire train of things. Thus we come, once more, to a Being above the Intellectual-Principle, and, since the sequent amounts to no less than the All, we recognize, again, a Being above the All (V – 3:11).

Plotinus contradicts himself in many passages, however, which seem to say that the One is not absolutely transcendent. He writes that the unity is, before everything else, to be solitary and self-existent and must be identified among the mass of other things as set apart from them; present to them, but distinguished from them (V – 6:3).

This contradiction can be clarified, however, with a closer look at the idea that God is goodness. If goodness is an attribute of God, does it mean that goodness exists apart from the nature and character of God? Of course not. Goodness is not a particular characteristic of God any more than beauty or holiness or mercy would be, but instead is a universal aspect of God, the very fiber of what it means to say God is to also be able to say God is Goodness, or Goodness is God. Goodness does not exist as the city of New York exists or as you exist, but nonetheless the measure of its reality is so high that in the Platonic system it is the all-embracing Idea.

If the idea of a Trinitarian understanding of Plotinus' hypostases is correct the One has no separate being apart from the two other Plotinian hypostases, and because it is the transcendent aspect of God transcendence can be logically separated from immanence. Plotinus does not bother himself with the metaphysical implications of transcendence and immanence simply because he does not force a dichotomy between the two.

Our preliminary conclusions then are that the One excludes the possibility that it is an independent Being and the One is an aspect of God - his transcendence.

## The One and Being, Thought and Purpose

Can we say of the One that it has Being? In other words, does it exist? Plotinus apparently denies it.

> It follows that the First must be without form, and, if without form, then it is no Being; Being must have some definition and therefore be limited; but the First cannot be thought of as having definition and limit, for thus it would be not the source but the particular item indicated by the definition assigned to it. If all things belong to the produced, which of them would you say belongs to the Supreme? Not included among them, this can be described only as transcending them: but they are Being and the Beings; it therefore transcends Being (V – 5:6).

If the passage above is taken at face value it appears Plotinus is saying that the One is what is often referred to in classical mysticism and oriental philosophy as *Nihil*, or nothingness. Yet, this conclusion is drawn only if the concepts of "Being" and "Reality" are confused.

For example, the reality of an entity is in converse relation to the measure of its being or existence. A particular stone exists, but the measure of its reality is no more than the slight measure proper to inanimate objects. Reality is an attribute of the universal, not of the particular.

What is Plotinus saying in this passage, then? He believes that the One is the ultimate Reality and that all other things are real only in so far as they share in the One. He is the source, and is a simplex "in which the multiplicity of the universe finds its coordinating factor." He transcends quality and is the source of all qualities and in the same way, 'being' or 'existence' is a secondary of which the one is the transcendent source.

The One does not have "Being" in the sense of *ousia* are substance, but according to Plotinus we cannot say that it lacks being, or is *nihil*, but we must say instead that it is "Being" that is "beyond Being." It is only through the *via negative* (through the negative, or in opposites) that we can speak of the One. Otherwise, we must be silent.

## Does the One Think?

The question of whether the One thinks must be raised in light of the present discussion. Common sense would dictate that this must be so, but Plotinus that an absolute simplex is above the idea of thinking or of being the subject or object of another entity's thoughts. This must be the case, for if it were not, a duality brings us back to the problems related to cause and effect. Plotinus writes:

> If the Good is simplex and without need, it can neither need the intellective act nor possess what it does not need: it will therefore not have intellection...The multiple must be always seeking its identity, desiring self-accord and self-awareness: but what scope is there within what is an absolute unity in which to move towards its identity? ... There exists the Good; ...and the intellective act may be defined as a movement towards the Good in some being that aspires toward it...Hence the Authentic Good has no need of intellection since itself and nothing else is good (V – 6:5).

Freedom, says Plotinus, is ascribed to a human being when action is in accord within the will of the agent. But sometimes we act in accordance with volition without being free. In Chapter Eight, we will further discuss the idea of freedom and free will between the One, the *Nous*, and the Soul. Can the attribute freedom be applied to the One in the same way as it is applied to human beings? Man is no simplex. Consequently even his free actions are predetermined by his environment, and that environment contrasts the person concerned.

## We Cannot Know the One

*How, then, do we ourselves come to be speaking of it? No doubt we deal with it, but we do not state it; we have neither knowledge nor intellection of it* (V – 3:14).

Like Plato before him, Plotinus ultimately concludes that Transcendent Being is not to be fully understood by the rational mind. Just as the idea of the Trinitarian God of Christian belief is often explained in terms of unfathomable mystery, the unity of the Plotinian godhead is not to be submitted to the particularity of human ontological processing.

To say that a particular table is red is to state one of the essential table-qualities it possesses, and this quality can be used in comparing and contrasting the table with qualities other tables have, which may or may not distinguish this particular table from the others (another table is white and so differentiated from this red one)..

Analysis like that in the example above makes obvious an understanding of the idea of *simpliciter*, a being or entity without extension in space and time, is outside of even the most uncomplicated human reasoning.

## Phases of the Human Psyche

*We do not, it is true, grasp it by knowledge, but that does not mean that we are utterly void of it; ...unable to state it, we may still possess it. . . Those divinely possessed and inspired have at least the knowledge that they hold some greater thing within them though they cannot tell what it is. It is above reason, mind and feeling; conferring these powers, not to be confounded with them* (V – 3:14).

Considering Plotinus' words here, then, it is important to distinguish, considering the difference between "possessing" and "stating" qualities about the One.

19

Plotinus helps here with a clear delineation of three phases or aspects contained in the human psyche:

1. Vegetative (animal)
2. Human (reason)
3. Divine (intuitive)

It would be safe to assume the last of these three phases would be the necessary portal to connection with the One. The following passage explains in detail:

> At the moment of touch there is no power whatever to make any affirmation; there is no leisure; reasoning on the vision is for afterwards. We may know we have had the vision when the Soul has suddenly taken light. This light is from the Supreme and is the Supreme; we may believe in the Presence when, like that other god on the call of a certain man, He comes bringing light: the light is the proof of the advent (V – 3:17)..

The Soul darkened by leisure, by human reasoning, cannot posses this vision. The ultimate goal for the Soul, according to Plotinus, is to seize this light emanating forth from the One and to realize it is this light which is itself the One. "Not by the light of any other principle - to see the Supreme which is also the means to the vision," will illuminate the Soul and allow it to see true reality "just as it is by the sun's own light that we see the sun."

## The One and Goodness

*Whatever may be said to be in need, is in need of a good and a preserver. Nothing can therefore be good to the One...It is a Beyond-Good, not even to itself a good but to such beings only as may be of quality to have part with it* (VI – 9:6).

What does it mean to say the one is "Beyond-Good?" Does Plotinus' idea of good compare to that of Plato already discussed? He describes the One as good in that all values, all ethical meaning in the realm of the *Nous* has its origin here, even though ethical value is not attributed to the One. He writes:

20

Just as the goodness of the Good is essential and not the outgrowth of some prior substance, so the Unity of the One is its essential. When we speak of the One and when we speak of the Good we must recognize an Identical Nature: we must affirm that they are the same (II – 9:1).

Because the One transcends existence, goodness in terms of human ethical value, in terms of the very fact that often man finds himself falling short of moral perfection, is simply the result of a separation from the One.

## The One as Unthinkable

Plotinus' One is not a separate entity from the *Nous* and the Soul. As simplex, logic cannot fathom or even pursue an understanding of the One except in terms of what in Platonic and Greek Orthodox philosophy is termed *apophaticism*. *Apophatic theology* consists in negating that which God is not – for example, God is not being itself. In the process of negation, then, God, or in Plotinus' case the One can be preserved as unknowable, inexpressible and incomprehensible.

This negative way of tradition, however, is balanced by a positive way known as *cataphaticism*, or *cataphatic theology*, which would say that God has revealed himself and has done so through Jesus Christ in a Trinitarian self-revealing. Plotinus resorts to cataphatic theology when he explains the One as being defined in terms of the *Nous*.

An appropriate example of this is Plotinus' argument that the One does not possess volition but is nevertheless free. Plotinus makes it clear that freedom is not an attribute of the One and that the One must be understood in the negative sense that there is no determining factor in respect of Him. The One is free because there is no environment. Plotinus says:

It is not, in our view, as an attribute that this freedom is present in the First...we apply to it the lesser terms brought over from lesser things and so tell it as best we may (VI – 8:8).

Ultra-reality, Plotinus' One is beyond the physical world, yet "emanates" (see Chapter Five) into reality to produce the *Nous* or the Divine Mind, which in turn overflows and from this overflow proceeds the Soul which generates the material world.

Four times in his life, Plotinus claimed to arrive at the highest reality of the One, to have come to a mystical union where reasoning abandons itself to pure relationship. His first-hand experience is the goal of the philosophy, Plotinus would say, to wake-up the slumbering spirit to a reality beyond the material world.

Plotinus' influence in history is, perhaps, the best witness to this awakening. This influence is recorded in the works of notables such as St. Augustine, Dante, Emerson and Tennyson and will be further explored in Chapter Ten. Regarding the present encounter with the nature and character of the One the great British poet, William Wordsworth (1770-1850), seems to best capture the mystical journey of the ancient sage in a portion of his *Ode on the Intimations of Immortality*, when he writes:

> Our birth is but a sleep and a forgetting:
> The soul that rises with us, our life's star,
> Hath elsewhere had its setting, and cometh from afar:
> Not in entire forgetfulness, and not in utter nakedness,
> But trailing clouds of glory do we come from God who is our home

Comparing Wordsworth to Plotinus similarities emerge:

> ...something transcendent: by a conversion towards the intellective art, it is loosed form the shackles and soars – when only it makes its memories the starting-point of a new vision of essential being (IV – 8:4).

It is an unfortunate fate, however, that this new vision of essential being must realize the "light of common day," an awareness of which Wordsworth writes and Plotinus' philosophy confronts. For it is true that "Heaven lies about us in our infancy!" even as "Shades of the prison-house begin to close upon the growing boy." It is in this stark realization of prodigal innocence desiring to return home that the reader of Plotinus seeks unity between the transcendence of the One and the struggle of the Soul striving for this unity. Here, at this still point of progress among these "shadowy recollections" at which Wordsworth hints, an understanding of the Plotinian *Nous* is sought.

# 3
# The *Nous*

*The intellect then is all real existences thought as not external to itself. They are neither prior nor subsequent to it, but it is, the primal lawgiver, or rather the law of existence. The saying is correct that thinking and existing are the same thing, and that the knowledge of immaterial entities is the same as the things themselves...For no real existence is outside the intellect or in space* (V − 9:5).

## A Philosophical Mistake

In the history leading up to the time of Plotinus the idea of the mind was always entangled with the idea of matter. Questions of whether the universe itself is simply one great mind or if mind is matter or *vice versa* (and if so does mind influence matter or does matter influence the mind?) were being asked.

At best it seemed obvious that there were some living organisms to be distinguished from others which had a peculiar consciousness of themselves and the world around them. These organisms were able to think, as it were, and to alter their environment to best suit them with an intelligence that appeared to go beyond instinctive patterns of behavior.

The relationship between thought (intelligence) and its relationship to matter (sense data) has interested philosophers for centuries. The primary question at hand is whether the mind as an entity of thought and sensory processing accomplishes both of these functions as a single process, or whether it is to be divided into one center which is responsible for higher cognitive processes such as reasoning and imagination and another center which through a complex series of neural networks and nerve fiber processes our physical sense experience. One can quickly speculate as to how such a division, if made, might set up the dichotomy between matter and non-matter, the crux of much of Plotinus' struggle to understand the connection between the One and the *Nous* and Soul.

23

In more modern times such philosophers as Thomas Hobbes, John Locke and David Hume have advanced an empirical theory of the mind, which has as its basic premise the idea that all that we can know is ultimately dependent on sense data. In the world of Plotinus and during the Middle Ages the idea that reality is dependent on the mind for the embodiment of its ideas and that no knowledge is possible without mental states was dominant and this ancient perspective was revived in modern times by philosophers such as Rene Descartes and Immanuel Kant.

We have already distinguished in Plato and Aristotle between the objects that are sensible (baseballs, apple pies, and Cabriolet) and those that are intelligible (math, souls, and God). Because these two distinct sets of objects can be recognized, it follows we must have some means of distinguishing between them – sense or intellect. Based on these observations, it is not an uncomfortable step to take which allows for an understanding of the characteristics of sense experience such as perception and imagination as being somehow unlike the powers of intellect such as reasoning and understanding. This distinction will be helpful in our study of Plotinus' concept of the *Nous*.

## A Prelude to the Plotinian *Nous*

Plotinus' realm of the One is "followed" by that of the Intellectual-Principle or Intelligence. This realm in his day often refers to the intellect, spirit or mind. Because these are all somewhat inadequate translations of "nous," the Greek word for intellect, reason, or mind, this monograph will substitute *Nous* where the Plotinian Intellectual-Principle is used.

A more detailed account of this history leading up to Plotinus is in order. Ranging from the idea that objects emanate images which the organ of sight lights upon (held by Democritus the Epicurean) to the possibility that the mind is composed of a fine textured matter which through divine spark, is the seat of the soul, the concept of the *Nous* is not without an illustrious history.

### The Greeks

The Greek philosopher of the day would have a difficult time trying to understand the modern day philosopher of mind's idea of *eliminitivism,* where mentalistic states such as belief and intention are explained away by theories of neurophysiology and empirical sciences.

Three well-known Greek thinkers appear to be especially concerned with positing a theory of the mind which also connects with a theory of the universe.

Anaximander (612-545 BC) held that the universe was composed of "the infinite," an eternal and imperishable substance and he used the idea of "eternal motion" to explain how the universe came to exist while Parmenides (515-445 BC) taught that the mind creates that which is not mind. He believed thought and existence are one and what cannot be thought cannot be and what cannot be cannot be thought. Anaxagoras (500-428 BC) taught a theory of motion which posits that the "nous" is responsible for movement and is the ultimate architect of everything which exists.

## *Plato and Aristotle*

Plato also referred to the mind as the soul on many occasions in his writings and the disembodied mind of his Theory of Forms contains the roots of knowledge before it is ever at home in the human body. The mind, however, is muddled and confused by the process of the birth of the flesh and the result is a forgetting of this innate knowledge. Learning then is a process of recollection and the proper methodology to be applied is that of bringing the student to the art of asking the right questions which will bring out the knowledge suppressed in the mind. Mind and matter are the stuff of the universe according to Plato, and the latter is a slave to the former.

Mind, for Aristotle, could not exist without matter and even the most rudimentary examples of matter, the lowest forms, possessed both form, content, and mind. Mind is both "pan-" and "panen-", both identical with matter and in and through all matter. Trace the evolution of matter from its lowest forms to its highest and the progression of an increasingly clearer picture of the ability of thought and knowledge will emerge, Aristotle believed.

## The Plotinian *Nous*

Roughly, the realm (hypostasis) of the Plotinian *Nous* corresponds to Plato's realm of ideas and to that of true being. Plato's Forms, however, are outside the *Nous* and self-sustaining and, in turn,

25

contemplated by the *Nous*. Ideas for Plotinus are God's thoughts and Intelligibles do not exist outside the Intelligence (V - 9:7; III - 9:1).

Another difference between Plato's ideal world and Plotinus' interpretation of it is an insistence on the individual's ability toward ideal, which immediately posits the question of how an infinity of individuals would result in an infinity of ideas. Here, Plotinus assumes that the sensible world is destroyed and regenerated again and in the process each new world contains the same indistinguishable individuals for which one idea would exist (see V - 7:1).

Plotinus' realm of ideas, again unlike that of Plato, also includes the existence of souls (see IV – 8:3). This doctrine creates a special problem. Take the ideal Socrates, unlike the soul of Socrates, must be composed of soul and body and the soul of the empirical Socrates should be only a copy of that of the ideal Socrates. Plotinus rejects the above consequence in some places of his writing (V - 9:13; VI - 4:14) and embraces it in others (III - 9:3; V - 2:1).

Regardless of Plotinus' often ambiguous and philosophically incoherent treatment of the *Nous*, he insists to the very end that it remains, like the One itself, and without multiplicity. Everything is contained in everything without losing its identity, just as in mathematics every theorem contains all the others and, thus, the totality of mathematics (V - 9:6, 9; IV - 3:2).

## Why the *Nous*?

*Why must there be something more than the Soul which will let us truly experience the One?*

In the first place, Plotinus says, there must be something more because the *Nous* and the *Soul* are different. In fact, *Nous* is superior to soul and what is better than something else, by its very nature must come before that something. He writes:

> Intellect is better, because soul does not as some think generate the intellect of her perfection. For how can the possible become actual, unless there be a cause which makes it actual? Were the process of actualization a matter of chance, perhaps the possible might not become actual (V – 9:4).

The *Nous*, as is the case with the One, is characterized by its perfection and unlike the Soul is in need of nothing to complete it. The Soul is viewed as matter which is formed and perfected by the *Nous*, just as parents bring the unruly child toward maturity over time. Soul is passible, says Plotinus, and because this is so there must be some impassible principle or all things would eventually come to destruction and fade into oblivion. He believes that because the soul is in the world, "there must be some principle outside the world, and this, too, must be prior to soul." For if what exists in the world exists in the corporeal and material, nothing there will preserve its identity (V – 9:4).

A careful reading of Plotinus' idea of the Nous will reveal that the idea of man and all matter in the universe is its non-eternal characteristic. This important observation will lead to the next consideration, that the *Nous* must exist prior to soul.

## Nous as Father to the Soul

The Soul is only an image of the intellect, says Plotinus. He uses examples of fire and words to explain what he means. As a thought expressed in words is an image of the thought in the Soul, so she is both the thought of the intellect and the entirety of its activity and the life which it sends forth to constitute a new form of being. An illustration of what I mean is fire which has both an inherent heat, and a heat which it radiates (V – 9:4).

A particularly endearing example of the *Nous* Plotinus offers is that of a father and a companion to the Soul, guiding it through stages of growth and maturity, leading it further up and farther into the Divine, the One. A separation between the two should not be made in this sense of relationship. He writes:

> Nor does anything separate them save the fact that they are different, inasmuch as the soul is one lower in rank and is the receptive principle, whereas the intellect is, as it were, the form. Still even the matter of the intellect is beautiful since it is intelligible and simple. And the excellence of the intellect can be clearly estimated by this superiority to soul (V – 1:3).

The Bible clearly states that the revelation of the existence of its God can be witnessed in the visible world:

27

From the creation of the world, God's invisible qualities, his eternal power and divine nature, have been clearly observed in what he made. As a result, people have no excuse (Romans 1:20).

Plotinus agrees that the excellence of the *Nous* can be reasoned in much the same way when one observes the beauty and grandeur of the phenomenal universe. Other distinguishing characteristics include the orderliness of its eternal motion and its spirits.

This observation alone should result in our advancing to a deeper understanding of archetypes far more lofty than those of the sense data we observe and, therefore result in the realization that there are things that are both incorruptible and eternal beyond the sensory world which we can know of through the *Nous*.

For the intellect comprehends everything that is immortal, every intellect, every god, every soul, in its eternal peace. Its peace, I say, for why should it in its felicity seek change? And into what could it change, seeing that it has all things of its own self (V – 1:4).

The *Nous* will not need to develop itself, according to Plotinus, because it exists in absolute perfection. Accordingly, everything that shares its existence will share in its perfect state, "possessed of nothing imperfect and nothing which is not the object of its thought."

## Nous as Present Reality

Such lofty thoughts, according to Plotinus, are possessions to those who pursue them which eliminate the need to search for them once discovered.

He writes a particularly moving passage regarding time's flow and its relationship to the *Nous*:

Rather is it eternally all things, and is the true eternity of which time encircling the soul is an image - time which leaves the old things behind and lays hold of new. For, to speak still of time, now one thing now another revolves about the soul, now Socrates, and now a horse, and always some single thing. The intellect, on the other hand, is all things. It contains all things in itself at rest within itself. Only the present exists for it, and is present eternally, and for it there is nothing future, since the future is already present to iti and nothing past. Nothing, I say, is past, but all realities have remained at rest there from eternity, as though content with them- selves as they are. Each of them is intellect and real existence, and the sum of them is all intellect and all real existence (V – 1:4).

The *Nous* thinks and in the act of thought produces existence, Plotinus says. Existence, in turn, is thought and gives thought and existence to the intellect. It isn't for the empiricist to try and understand exactly what he means by existence giving thought to the *Nous* in this way as the idea of course remains beyond the logical and in the realm of the possible.

Regardless, Plotinus believes that existents are caused by something else - they exist simultaneously and never desert one another – because together they form the *Nous* and existence. Thinking and thought are one and where thinking there too is identity and difference.

## *Nous as First Principle*

Not to be confused with the One as First Principle, the first principles Plotinus refers to are his version of Plato's Forms. They are the *Nous*, existence, difference, and identity. He also includes the categories of motion and rest among these, motion in regards to thinking and rest for the principle of identity. Without difference or differentiation thought could not exist, nor an object on which to think of or about. Without difference unity would not be a possibility for unity requires diversity to define it.

The ideas are self-identical, have a common element, yet also differ from each other and because of the plurality that results quantity can be measured. Quality, on the other hand, Plotinus says, "is generated by the fact that each one of these principles from which all else proceeds has its peculiar and proper character (V – 9:5)."

## *Nous "in actu"*

*Nous* it is to be understood, is not potential knowledge or knowledge which comes from acquisition. If it were, Plotinus points out, it would be outside of itself, incomplete:

…we should have to seek for yet another intellect prior to this. By intellect we are to understand that which is intellect *in actu* (in motion), and eternally. But if its thought be not imported from without, when it thinks anything it must itself be the occasion of its thought, and when it ix possessed of any object be the occasion of that possession. But if it be the occasion and source of its thought, it will itself be the object of its thought (V – 9:5).

The essence of the *Nous* and the object of its thought are inseparable though we often think of them as not. If essence and the object of its thought were separate, essence would become an unintelligible object of potential, not actual existence.

Again this can be confusing in consideration of how the *Nous* thinks and acts. Plotinus explains that because it is real existence, the *Nous* will think and support the world of real existences, what is at other times referred to as the ideas. The *Nous* is the sum total of the ideas and thinks of them as existing either elsewhere than in itself, or in itself as its own nature.

The *Nous* thinks of the Ideas as composing its own nature and existing within its very nature, Plotinus believes. He concludes that "…the seat of the form is not the sensible object as some think. For in no case is the primary and fundamental the phenomenal. The form in sensible objects imposed upon matter is an image of real existence, and every form in objects comes from something without, refers thither, and is an image thereof (V – 9:5)."

## Nous Prior to Existence

The One, as creator of all things, does not think of what does not exist in order to create what does exist, Plotinus says. Forms or ideas are pre-existent and are the archetypes, the very essence of the *Nous*. He writes:

If some people talk of seminal reasons (providing a basis for new research) as sufficient, evidently they must be talking of the eternal reasons. But if the reasons are eternal and impassible, they must exist in an intellect, and in an intellect such that it is prior to conditioned existence, nature, and soul, seeing that these have a potential existence (V – 9:5).

30

The *Nous*, Plotinus repeats, exists in itself eternally in itself, is immutable (cannot change), cannot be destroyed and, therefore, constitutes real existence. Phenomena (intelligibles) have their existence as objects which can be defined and must participate in this real existence.

For example, consider that artist's bronze or the carpenter's pine as both symbolizing the doorways by which the creator enters into the creation of statue or furniture. At the same time, Plotinus says, the arts themselves remain outside of matter in their self-identity, and contain the true statue and the true bed (V – 9:5).

This is also true of corporeal things, Plotinus says that the difference between images and real existences is shown this universe which participates in images. The intelligible world real existences are immutable (whereas the things of this world are mutable). Real existences, being without extension, reside in themselves without need of space and have an intellectual and self-sufficient kind of existence.

Images need to be preserved by something outside of them, while the *Nous*, "which with its wonderful nature supports what naturally tends to fall, itself seeks no support."

## *Nous as Real Existence*

The *Nous* is real existence and all the real existences are contained within it. It does not factor down to a spatial explanation, however, but one which has been already best explained in the relationship of the One to the *Nous*. All things between the *Nous* and the Soul exist in coherence but, as such, remain distinguished from one another.

> For the soul also is possessed of many notions at the same time, without confusing them. Each does its proper work at the proper time without involving the others. So, too, each thought has a pure activity drawn from the thoughts which lie within it. After this fashion, and to a far greater extent, the intelligible universe is all things together and yet not together inasmuch as each real existence is an individual and peculiar power. But the whole intellect includes them as a genus contains its species, or as a whole its parts (V – 9:6).

Plotinus believes that whatever objects we can see in the phenomenal world are also contained in the world of the *Nous* and there is nothing contrary to nature in the coming together of the two: Just as there is nothing contrary to art in the arts, nor for that matter lameness in the seed, seeing that lameness arises during growth from the failure of the seminal reason to overcome matter, and is a chance mutilation of form.

In the world of the *Nous* all qualities, quantities, numbers, magnitudes, conditions, actions, natural properties, motions and rests, both in whole and in part are in harmony. It is a world where time is replaced by eternity and space can only be understood in terms of infinity to the "nth" power.

# 4
# The Soul

*We see the sun and the moon and the other stars shifting place and course in an ordered progression. It is therefore within reason that the souls, also, should have their changes, not retaining unbrokenly the same quality, but ranged in some analogy with their action and experience – some taking rank as head and some as foot in a disposition consonant with the Universal Being which has its degrees in better and less good. A soul, which neither chooses the highest that is here, nor has lent itself to the lowest, is one which has abandoned another, a purer, place, taking this sphere in free election* (IV – 4:45).

## The Notion of the Soul

Is the soul composed of the finest and purest fire atoms, or is it very thin and rarefied air? When a person dies does the soul go from that body to another body, or does it go to a place of shades and forms to pine away for the world of men? These are the sorts of questions the philosophers of antiquity were asking.

Plotinus' idea of Soul, particularly addressed during his middle period, is certainly multi-faceted and varied in its many roles. In the visible world, bodies are formed or created through Soul. This is perhaps the bottom level of its use if a hierarchy is considered. At its highest level, the Plotinian Soul mingles with the *Nous* and transcends the visible world to join with the One.

In a mystical grammar of ascent, Plotinus attempts to come to terms with the Soul's rise to the One despite its embodiment by formulating a doctrine of the Soul which is not cut off from the rigors of practical initiative - required to raise the Soul, through philosophical reflection, beyond worldly matters. It is often with great difficulty and lengthy study the student of Plotinus manages to articulate in terms of a meaningful explanation the distinctions existing between Soul and *Nous* in Plotinus' works.

# A Prelude to the Plotinian Soul

People are born, they grow, struggle, dream, plan, and build, only to surrender at last to death. To the human mind surveying history the demise of the body has always marked a swift and certain closing, for inevitably the body will decay, disintegrate, and disappear, so that, in time, every trace of its existence is gone.

But the human mind has never let the story end at the grave. Certainly throughout history, the majority of the once living asked the burning questions: Is there something more beyond the last breath? Is there more to man than his time on earth? Could there be some sort of soul that carried on beyond a life in space and time?

## *Immortality or Eternality?*

From time immemorial peoples from all cultures held fast to the belief of the immortality of the soul, an "after" life which robbed death of its sting. But whatever measure of immortality attributed to the soul, the matter of eternality was something different. Upon dying, many primitive cultures believed, the soul left the body but did not travel beyond this life; instead remaining near to its former habitation it might often return to the burial sight if only to enjoy a veritable feast of food and drink graciously prepared for it by those yet living.

Metempsychosis, transmigration, reincarnation, the passing of an eternal soul at death from its body to another body, teaching often associated with Eastern religious practices most often tethered the movement of the soul from one body to the next to ethical standards practiced in the original life - good works warranted entrance into a better body and bad works had the adverse result.

## *Early Greek Notions*

Long before Plotinus entertained various notions of the soul including that of reincarnation the Greeks were also concerned with a variety of theories.

For example, Pythagoras (570-494 BC) believed the destiny of the soul upon leaving the body hinged on the life lived while the body was still alive. Complex guidelines to follow were implemented to make certain death would not rob its victim of an after-life of desirable conditions. Another Greek philosopher, Anaximenes (545 BC) believed that a sort of rarefied air composed the soul and kept the person together and when this "thin air" left the body disintegration set in and the body was destroyed. Democritus (460-371 BC), on the other hand, believed that like the world itself the soul was composed of the most perfect fire atoms – imagine a soul atom placed between two other atoms in the body – and that as long as a person is alive the lungs breathe soul atoms in and out. When the body dies, he taught, these soul atoms mingle with the rest of the atoms of the universe.

## Plato and Aristotle

There is a "World Soul" according to Plato and this is to be distinguished from the individual souls of mortals. Souls exist before they enter bodies and are eternal gifts from the Demiurge who composes and maintains both the World Soul and the soul of the individual. Like the idea of enlightenment in Eastern philosophy, the soul must set its sights on delivering itself from the many traps the flesh will inevitably prepare if it is to experience the pure ideas of the Theory of Forms and its eternal significance.

Aristotle believed the soul is both in and through all matter and the only obvious difference between the soul of a woman and the soul of an asparagus is simply the fact that the woman can think and conceptualize many different ways to cook asparagus for dinner that would be both emotionally and intellectually uplifting whereas the asparagus cannot, as far as she knows, even begin to reason in such a way. Creative reason of the sort this particular woman is exhibiting, however, does not have its origin in her mind but has in fact existed before the creation of bodies or souls. It is out-sourced, so to say, to the one Divine mind and naturally, when the body dies, the only part of the soul that carries on is that which returns to God.

## The Universal Soul

The *Fourth Ennead*, consisting of the *Third* and *Fourth Tractate*, consists of a progression of questions Plotinus asks and attempts to illuminate regarding a Platonist theory of the Soul over and against his own developing theory.

The progression can be discussed in terms of six questions. First, what of the relationship of the individual souls to the All-Soul (they can be neither parts nor yet separate)? (IV – 3:1-8). Second, what of the

35

problem attending the entry of souls into bodies? (IV – 3:9-18). Third, what of the situation of the embodied soul, its divisions, and its fate after leaving the body? (IV – 3:19-24). Fourth, what of memory? What sort of memory, and so what continuity of personality, can there be in disembodied souls? (IV – 3:25 to IV – 4:5). Fifth, what of memory as regarding planetary gods or the earth? (IV – 4:6-17). Sixth, what of the experience and activities of the embodied soul? (IV – 4:18-29).

Plotinus asks the question, "On what subject can we more reasonably expend the time required by minute discussion and investigation?," specifically regarding the notion of the soul; a "matter" he writes "well worth attention." This chapter, while not exhausting his expertise regarding all of the questions above, is an attempt to introduce the major themes several of the questions ask. No particular order, such as that observed by MacKenna, will be observed in the process of gathering this insight.

## The "All-Soul"

It has been rightly noted that in regards to mortality every cradle swings over an open grave. Birth like death, for Plotinus, at least as it regards the Soul, does not signal an end to earthly life. Like a swinging door birth and death are merely passageways, portals as it were, connecting the eternal and finite worlds. It is the body of flesh and bone, one day present the next swallowed by death, which in its transience acts as a vehicle transporting the Soul from unity with the One to (dis)-unity and multiplicity, and back again to the One.

Plotinus' Soul is divided into three parts, or aspects:

1. Transcendent higher All-Soul
2. Immanent but separate lower All-Soul
3. Particular Soul that gives life and reality to material things

The All-Soul encompasses the Soul of each one of us. Another way to say this is there is a spark, or part, of the divine whole in each individual Soul. For Plotinus, this spark can be nurtured through contemplation a Soul can experience union with the All-Soul because of the divine spark within rising up to meet its source. It can also be nurtured with a proper attitude and spiritual orientation, the embodied soul will rise inevitably. However, if through diversion the body turns back on itself, the material world is as a prison, isolating the Soul from ascending the way of truth leading it back to the All-Soul.

As the saying goes, "No man is an island." For Plotinus the euphemism is of particular relevance where he describes the very heart of man's rebellion against the One in terms of estrangement and isolation.

## A Turning Away

Space and time are not constraints regarding the arduous journey of the Soul to its union with the One, according to Plotinus. He writes:

But it is admitted that all souls are like, and are entities; clearly, soul is not subject to part in the sense in which magnitudes are: our opponents themselves would not consent to the notion of the All-Soul being whittled down into fragments, yet this is what they would be doing, annulling the All-Soul – if any collective soul existed at all – making it a mere piece of terminology, thinking of it like wine separated into many portions, each portion, in its jar, being described as a portion of the total thing, wine (IV[2] – 3:2).

Once again, the intermingling of *Nous* and Soul play a prominent role in Plotinus teaching. Embodied, the Soul does not cease to inhabit the realm of the *Nous* completely. The highest or most exalted aspect of the individual Soul remains indwelling the realm of the *Nous*. Though rare, even in this state of embodiment, the Soul can struggle to experience moments of transcendence from the lower to the higher realms of unity. Plotinus describes, at one point, what he calls the "unit soul," experiencing such a journey:

The unit soul (it may be conceived) holds aloof, not actually falling into body: the differentiated souls – the All-Soul, with the others – issue from the unity while still constituting, within certain limits, an association. They are one soul by the fact that they do not belong unreservedly to any particular being; they meet, so to speak, fringe to fringe; they strike out here and there, but are held together at the source much as light is a divided thing upon earth, shining in this house and that, and yet remains uninterruptedly one identical substance (IV[1] – 3:4).

The Soul, argues Plotinus, can claim immortality only if it is itself an emanation of a source which can make the same declaration. Infinite regress, a traveling back through a time continuum without arriving at a cause or source for the effect, is not an option for Plotinus. Such a regress must inevitably yield an immortal substance of some sort begetting, or depositing, the many and various multiples which exist both through and beyond itself.

## The Soul Inhabiting Body

How does the Soul come to inhabit the body? Plotinus believes it enters the body under two forms (IV -3:9):

1. *Metensomatosis* – the entry of a soul present in body by change from one (wholly material) frame to another, or the entry of a soul leaving an aerial or fiery body for one of earth.
2. Entry from the wholly bodiless into any kind of body; this is the earliest from of any dealing between body and soul.

Plotinus uses words such as "entry" and "ensoulment" to describe the process of these forms. Exactly how such ensoulment occurs proves to be quite abstract in explanation.

While the Soul (as an eternal, a Divine Being) is at rest – in rest firmly based on Repose, the Absolute – yet, as we may put it, that huge illumination of the Supreme pouring outwards comes at last to the extreme bourne of its light and dwindles to darkness; this darkness, now lying there beneath, the Soul sees and by seeing brings to shape; for in the law of things this ultimate depth, neighboring with soul, may not go void of whatsoever degree of that Reason-Principle it can absorb, the dimmed reason of reality at its faintest (IV – 3:9).

A stately mansion built be an Architect who inhabits the Absolute realm serves as an example for Plotinus' explanation of the entry of soul into body:

He has judged [the mansion] worthy in all its length and breadth of all the care that can serve its Being – as far as it can share in Being – or to its beauty, but a care without burden to its director, who never descends, but presides over it from above: this gives the degree in which the Cosmos is ensouled, not be a soul belonging to it, but by one present to it; it is mastered, not master; not possessor, but possessed. The Soul bears it up, and it lies within, no fragment of it unsharing (IV – 3:9).

## The Soul's Rebirth

The Soul is immortal, the very essence of life, and man, animal and material object are a part of the Soul in different degrees. The concept of reincarnation enters into Plotinian philosophy as a description of the Soul passing from one body to another.

Plotinus uses the following lengthy example to explain himself:

It comes to no more than the murder of one of the persons in a play; the actor alters his make-up and enters in a new role. The actor, of course, was not really killed; but if dying is but changing a body as the actor changes a costume, or even an exit from the body like the exit of the actor from the boards when he has no more to say or do - though he will return to act on another occasion - what is there so very dreadful in this transformation of living beings one into another? Surely this is better than if they had never existed; that would mean the bleak quenching of life, precluded from passing outside itself; . . . Thus every man has his place, a place that fits the good man, a place that fits the bad: each within the two orders of men makes his way, naturally, reasonably, to the place, good or bad, that suits him, and takes the position he has made his own. There he talks and acts, in blasphemy and crime or in all goodness; for the actors bring to this play what they were before it was ever staged (VI – 9:8).

Similar to the doctrine of *karma* in Hinduism and Buddhism, where the effect of a person's actions during successive phases of the person's existence are regarded as determining the person's destiny, a person is tied to his past in Plotinian philosophy and the Soul moving from body to body is subject to accountability regarding it's actions at every stage.

Plotinus has us imagine a man, who was once a ruler, being forced into slavery due to an abuse of his power. This fall, however, will eventually lead to this man's future good. The point is of course that whoever misuses power will be made poor and that poverty is not a problem for the good person but delivers the proud Soul from vanity and foolishness. "It is not an accident that makes a man a slave; no one is a prisoner by chance; every bodily outrage has its due cause. The man once did what he now suffers (VI – 9:8)."

When the body dies, the Soul returns to the One. If the Soul is too engrossed in the cares of the world, if the body holds it in its snare, it will not recognize the will of the One and will be held to the earth in a cycle of reincarnation.

## A Grammar of Ascent

After what fashion, then, is the one essence in the many Souls? There are two possibilities Plotinus assumes:

1.  The One essence in them all is a sum total.
2.  The many are derived from the whole and single essence without disturbing its wholeness or unity.

There shouldn't be a problem understanding, according to Plotinus, that the many Souls are related to the One as the one unity which offers itself to the many, and simultaneously does not exhaust itself in this offering. It is able to do this and remain one because it can penetrate all things simultaneously and not be splintered into multiplicity.

For example, take the idea of science as a discipline. It is related to all of its parts in such a manner that its relation is not impaired by the derivation of such parts. In the Soul, says Plotinus, all the parts coexist in their actuality:

> In the case of a science, to revert, each part is ready to which you may wish to put your hand. The readiness for use lies in the part, but it gets its efficacy from its contiguity to the whole. One cannot regard it as empty of the other propositions. Were it, it would not hold either in practice or in theory, but would be mere child's prattle (IV – 9:5).

Such as analogy applies to an understanding of the Soul's relation both the body and the *Nous*.

The material universe is ordered by the Soul, but not on an external level like a surgeon operating on a patient to fix an ailment but

40

from the inside instead. However, the Soul is not immanent in terms of being confined by space. It is outside of both memory and action:

> The Soul which still drags a burden will tell of all the man did and felt; but upon death there will appear, as time passes, memories of the lives lived before, some of the events of the most recent life being dismissed as trivial…but with lapse of time it will come to forgetfulness of many things that were mere accretion. Then, free and alone at last, what will it have to remember (IV – 3:27)?

As a tree grows from the seed, the universe emerges from the Soul spontaneously, and as the Soul contemplates the *Nous*, it reflects back upon the created order the laws which govern the universe. Soul, in turn, emerges out of the *Nous*' contemplation of the One, and any action it has toward the body is in response to its understanding of the action of *Nous* upon itself in contemplation of the One.

## The Soul's Descent Into the Body

In one of his most oft quoted passages, Plotinus writes of his own encounter with what in modern day language would be called an "out-of-body experience." It has happened to him more than once:

> Lifted out of the body into myself; becoming external to all other things and self-encentered; beholding a marvelous beauty; then, more than ever, assured of community with the loftiest order; enacting the noblest life, acquiring identity with the divine; stationing within It by having attained that activity; poised above whatsoever within the Intellectual is less than the Supreme: yet, there comes the moment of descent from intellection to reasoning, and after that sojourn in the divine, I ask myself how it happens that I can now be descending, and how did the soul ever enter into my body, the soul which, even within the body, is the high thing it has shown itself to be (IV – 8:1,3).

This descent of the Soul into the body and the place of the *Nous*, Plotinus calls the "Intellectual Kosmos," and it is here where the intellective powers, the separate intelligences, are no longer merely one but are the one and many. In this place there are many souls and the one is the true source of the "differing many just as from one genus there rise various species, better and worse, some of the more intellectual order, others less effectively so (IV – 8:1,3)."

It is also in the descent that the Soul confronts a profound contradictoriness. Plotinus writes:

> Everywhere we hear of [the Soul] in bitter and miserable durance in body, a victim to troubles and desires and fears and all forms of evil, the body its prison or its tomb, the kosmos its cave or cavern. Now this does not clash with the first theory [that of the impassivity of soul as in the All]; for the descent of the human Soul has not been due to the same causes [as that of the All-Soul] (IV – 8:1,3).

This "bitter and miserable durance in body," is the heart of the mystical search for the secret stairway which leads a body tired of wandering and a mind confused of thinking up and out of the dark wound of the knowledge of fear, inadequacy and failure, both internal and external.

Plotinus believes it is possible to reconcile all these apparent contradictions. However, such reconciliation requires a fierce succession of choices on the individual's part which will not usually be considered until the very essence of the grief which follows the descent of the soul into the body is distilled. This is despair realized and manifests itself as a state of drab petty meanness and complete disregard for pleasing the One.

Such misfortune, according to Plotinus, need never occur in the first place, however. For a Soul which has never "deeply penetrated the body" will never suffer the trials of the slave to the body. It can remain a sovereign Soul ruling over the body's dangerous needs, ruling over potential shortcomings and allowing no ground for the growth of misplaced desire or fear.

## Are All Souls One?

For Plotinus, the sovereign Soul is the sensitive Soul if it is aware of unity in itself and others, and the bitter Soul remains calloused in its multiplicity. Yet, all Souls are one in the sense that they are connected to the universe which is under the sovereign control of the One. He explains in another of his most widely read passages from the *Fourth Ennead* regarding the question of whether or not all Souls are one:

...we to hold similarly that your soul and mine and all are one, and that the same thing is true of the universe, the soul in all the several forms of life being one soul, not parceled out in separate items, but an omnipresent identity? That one identical soul should be virtuous in me and vicious in someone else is not strange: it is only saying that an identical thing may be active here and inactive there (IV – 9:1,3,4).

In this active and inactive omnipresent identity Plotinus posits, he is not trying to argue for the negation of multiplicity in the unity of all Souls one with another but, as we have seen earlier in our understanding of the hypostases relation to each other "we are thinking of soul as simultaneously one and many," he writes, "participant in the nature divided in body, but at the same time a unity by virtue of belonging to that Order which suffers no division (IV – 9:3)."

Plotinus uses himself to explain how, for example, a part of his body might be experiencing a particular sensation at a given moment but the effect of such might not occur to his entire person. On the other hand, if in his higher faculties (here he must be referring reasoning) he is aware of something, all of him must be aware. He writes:

...in the same way any influx from the All upon the individual will have manifest effect since the points of sympathetic contact are numerous...Yet, looking at another set of facts, reflection tells us that we are in sympathetic relation to each other, suffering, overcome, at the sight of pain, naturally drawn to forming attachments; and all this can be due only to some unity among us (IV – 9:3).

A variety of powers under the class of sensory-perceptive experience spread across the multiplicity of Souls and divided among bodies does not conflict with unity, according to Plotinus. The "seed contains many powers and yet it is one thing," he writes. From this unity comes a variety that is unity.

# 5

# On Emanation and Union

Plotinus uses the words "emanation" and "effulgration" to explain the relationship of the three hypostasis to one another; the One to the *Nous* and the *Nous* to the Soul. This particular doctrine is one of the most difficult to understand, especially the aspect which concerns how each of the hypostasis in the process of emanating (sending forth) its substance itself remains undiminished.

Plotinus writes in the *Sixth Tractate* of the *Fifth Ennead*:

> Given this immobility in the Supreme, it can neither have yielded assent nor uttered decree nor stirred in any way towards the existence of a secondary. What happened then? What are we to conceive as rising in the neighbourhood of that immobility? It must be a circumradiation – produced from the Supreme but from the Supreme unfaltering – and may be compared to that brilliant light encircling the sun and ceaselessly generated from that unchanging substance (V – 1:6)

In the *Eighth Tractate* of the *Third Ennead* he writes:

> We conclude that this Being is limitless and that in all the outflow from it there is no lessening, either in its emanation, since this also is the entire universe, nor in itself, the starting point, since it is no assemblage of parts (to be diminished by any outgoing source) (III – 8:8).

Finally, in the *Ninth Tractate* of the *Sixth Ennead* he writes:

> In this choiring (union), the soul looks upon the wellspring of Life, wellspring also of Intellect, beginning of Being, fount of Good, root of Soul. It is not that these are poured out from the

44

Supreme, lessening it as if it were a thing of mass. At that the emanants would be perishable; but they are eternal; they spring from an eternal principle, which produces them not by its fragmentation but in virtue of its intact identity: therefore they too hold firm; as long as the sun shines, there will be light (VI – 9:9).

It is clear from these passages that the emanating entity remains outside as the source but is also present in its destination. As Plotinus says, it is "outside of place, and reason tells us that it will be present entire and that, present to the total, it must be present in the same completeness to every several unity (VI – 4:3)." Or, as in VI – 9:7, "…this Principle does not lie away somewhere leaving the rest void; to those of power to reach, it is present; to the inapt, absent."

This "circumradiation" which he speaks of, comparing the immobility of the Supreme to the rippled circles of light surrounding the sun, this reference to the limitlessness of the One which knows of no "lessening" in its emanation and possesses no parts like a product in an assembly line, all of these references Plotinus gathers to offer a deeper understanding of what emanation actually is.

The Simplex must exist before all things. It is "self-gathered," "not interblended" with the forms it creates, Plotinus would say, and yet somehow it is able to be present to these forms (V – 4:1, 11).

To the divine mystery of the One's emanation into a plurality of creation Plotinus will only speak in positive terminology of such a praiseworthy event which not only serves to rescue multiplicity moving toward chaos from itself but also offers the One a chance to actualize the awesome character contained within itself.

## *Nous* and Soul

Does the One create the *Nous*, or is the *Nous* merely a kind of self-reflection of the One? Plotinus says the One faces itself and in doing so sees itself; this self-reflection ("circumradiation") is, or begets, *Nous*:

This greatest, later than the divine unity, must be the Divine Mind, and it must be the second of all existence, for it is that which sees The One on which alone it leans while the First has no need whatever of it (V – 1:7).

45

The *Nous* receives identity from the act itself, too – that is, the act of turning back and contemplating the One:

> ...that vision directed upon the One establishes the Nous; standing towards the One to the end of vision, it is simultaneously Nous and Being; and, attaining resemblance in virtue of this vision, it repeats the act of the One in pouring forth a vast power (V – 2:1).

The Soul is born out of this vast power and is sustained by turning toward the *Nous* as its source, but it cannot possibly achieve the level of perfection as its source and as a result experiences multiplicity striving for unity.

Matter is the emanation of the Soul. It must be indeterminate, lacking clarity or precision, Plotinus says, not alive or in any way imaging the Soul (III - 4:1). In Chapter Five the levels of the Soul - higher, lower, lowest - were explained. Matter is the lowest of these, the physical world and the Soul, comparable to Plato's Demiurge, is the architect of matter.

## *The Soul's Descent*

The Soul, says Plotinus, "has lost it innocency of conducting the higher which it knew when it stood with the All-Soul." Here he describes emanation of Soul and even *Nous* in terms of their "falling away" from the "All-Soul" and unity with the One.

The *Nous* reflects upon itself and does not desire the One: "...since the souls are of the *Nous*, and the Supreme even loftier, we understand that contact is otherwise procured...(VI – 9:8).

The Soul reflects upon itself and wants to rule the world, thus to turn away from the *Nous* and to the body which will accomplish its selfish desire: "So it is with the individual souls; the appetite for the divine *Nous* urges them to return to their source, but they have, too, a power apt to administration in this lower sphere (IV – 8:4).

Matter emanates from Soul as the result of the Soul's wish to belong to itself (III – 9:3). The "lowest" kind of Soul (the vegetative) is called the most foolhardy: "...what is there is one phase, the more rebellious and less intellectual, outgone to that extreme... (V – 2:2)."

Is it more proper then, when speaking of Plotinus' emanation between hypostasis, to discuss this ebb and flow as one of a falling away and a returning? Both, perhaps, but in either case the intimate

46

connections between hypostasis require definition in temporal terms in a collision with transcendent terms.

Incarnation, the Soul's constitution in the human body trapped in time and space now searching for the One and escape into the realm of unity it offers, is the nexus of the underlying confusion.

## Incarnation

The Soul can never completely fall away from the *Nous* or the *Nous* from the One, Plotinus explains:

> And – if it is desirable to venture the more definite statement of a personal conviction with the general view – even our human Soul has not sunk entire; something of it is continuously in the Intellectual Realm, though if that part, which is in this sphere of sense, hold the mastery, or rather be mastered here and troubled, it keeps us blind to what the upper phase holds in contemplation (IV – 8:8).

As a result of the Soul's incarnation (the immanent but separate lower All-Soul) it is placed in relation to a body it must escape from in order to return to its proper place of dwelling. Plotinus writes:

> No doubt the individual body – though in all cases appropriately placed within the universe – is of itself in a state of dissolution, always on the way to its natural terminus, demanding much irksome forethought to save it from every kind of outside assailant, always gripped by need, requiring every help against constant difficulty...(IV – 8:2).

The body gripped by the Transcendent Universal Soul or "World-Soul" is "complete, competent, self-sufficing," and "exposed to nothing contrary to its nature." This Transcendent Soul may still occupy the body, Plotinus says, but it will not be governed by it nor will it be wrested "from its own sure standing in the highest (IV – 8:8)."

## Beholder and Beheld

*The holy things may not be uncovered to the stranger, to any that has not attained to see. There was not two; beholder was one with beheld; it was not a vision compassed but a unity apprehended. The man or woman formed by this mingling with the Supreme must – if they only remember – carry its image impressed upon them: they have become the Unity, nothing within or without inducing any diversity; no movement now, no passion, no outlooking desire, once this ascent is achieved...* (VI – 9:11)

In the presence of such "rule of Mysteries," Plotinus accords, "Nothing [is] Divulged to the Uninitiate," and there is no common story to describe the Supreme. Of highest priority to Plotinus is the problem how the One, in spite of its being ineffable (incapable of being expressed, unspeakable), can be known. In the pseudo-Platonic Epinomis (992B), the author insists that in order to know the One (whatever "knowledge" means here), the soul must itself become one; the Platonic Letters also seem to teach some kind of suprarational insight.

Perhaps starting from passages such as these and also from passages in Aristotle in which some kind of infallible knowledge of certain objects is described as a kind of touching, Plotinus asserts that to "know" the One means to become one with it, which the soul can accomplish only by becoming as simple or as "alone" as the One.

In the moment of such a union the soul has become God or, rather, is God; the soul has reascended to its original source:

Our being is the fuller for our turning Thither; this is our prosperity; to hold aloof is loneliness and lessening. Here is the soul's peace, outside of evil, refuge taken in the place clean of wrong; here it has its Act, its true knowing; here it is immune. Here is living, the true; that of today, all living apart from Him, is but a shadow, a mimicry. Life in the Supreme is the native activity of Intellect; in virtue of that silent converse it brings forth gods, brings forth beauty, brings forth righteousness, brings forth all moral good; for of all these the soul is pregnant when it has been filled with God. This state is its first and its final, because from God it comes, its good lies There, and, once turned to God again, it is what it was. Life here, with the things of earth, is a sinking, a defeat, a failing of the wing (VI -9:9).

Among the terms Plotinus uses to describe this condition are "ecstasy," "simplicity," "self-surrender," "touching," and "flight of the

48

alone to the alone" (VI - 9:3, 11). This ecstasy - repeatedly experienced by Plotinus himself - is undoubtedly the climactic moment of man's life. It is not expressible in words; only he who has experienced it knows what it means to be ravished away and full of God.

An example from the modern Judeo-Christian mystical tradition may enlarge our understanding of Plotinus. Thomas Merton (1915-1968), a Trappist monk, entered Gethsemane Abbey in Kentucky at age 26 and dedicated his life toward an initiation into the divine union of man with God. Merton writes of a particular encounter where, at the end of himself, his mind receives the mystical speech of God:

> *I will lead you into solitude. I will lead you by the way that you cannot possibly understand, because I want it to be the quickest way...You will be praised, and it will be like burning at the stake. You will be loved, and it will murder your heart and drive you into the desert...And when you have been praised a little and loved a little I will take away all your gifts and all your love and all your praise and you will be utterly forgotten and abandoned and you will be nothing, a dead thing, a rejection. And in that day you shall begin to possess the solitude you have so long desired. And your solitude will bear immense fruit in the souls of men you will never see on earth.* [1]

In this passage it is as if Merton's God is leading him toward non-being, to a place where the soul is utterly rejected and abandoned in order to receive, in turn, a new orientation. Plotinus speaks of this place as the "Principle to Essence." It is the place where the mortal soul (Principle in Action) suddenly recognizes that the One is "Beyond-Essence," beyond being, and is not only the generator of Essence but is neither subject to Essence or Himself. In this place of non-being Merton speaks of, there is space to realize that the One has no need of being, even though He is responsible for bringing such being about.

Like Plotinus, Merton argues that man lost his immortality, his contemplation, his power over himself and over irrational creation and finally even his status as a companion of God. Along with this he lost his immunity from disordered passion, his freedom from ignorance, his incapacity to suffer, his ability to recognize the true character and nature of the Beheld, the Supreme Being.

He lost his immortality? Why? Merton writes:

Because for him, life consisted precisely in his union with God the source of life, and left to his own contingency, he himself became his own source of life. But he was a deficient source that soon ran dry.[2]

Man (Merton's "first Adam" regarding the Christian story of his fall from communion with God) lost his freedom, too: not his freedom of choice, but his freedom from sin, his freedom to attain without obstacle to that love for which he had been created. He exchanged the spontaneity of a perfectly ordered nature elevated by the highest gifts of mystical grace, for the compulsions and anxieties and weaknesses of a will left to itself, a will which does what it does not want to do, hates what it ought to love and avoids what it ought to seek with its whole being.

For the reascent to God man prepares himself by the acquisition of all the perfections, virtues in Plotinus' language, "living an incorruptible life" in Merton's Christian theology. However, for Plotinus, each of these perfections acquires different meanings according to the level on which man's spiritual life takes place - thus, there is a social fairness, above it another kind of fairness, and so on. Man also prepares himself by the exercise of dialectics:

But what is escape? In attaining Likeness to God,' we read. And this is explained as 'becoming just and holy, living by wisdom,' the entire nature grounded in Virtue $(I - 2:1)$.

The preliminary stages of achievement Plotinus calls "becoming Godlike," a condition often described by Platonists preceding Plotinus as the ultimate goal of Plato's philosophy. This becoming is paradoxical, however. It requires withdrawal in order to advance. The "loveliness" of the Soul sought by the pilgrim who wishes to progress in beauty is first the way of regress:

Withdraw into yourself and look. And if you do not find yourself beautiful yet, act as does the creator of a statue that is to be made beautiful: he cuts away here, he smoothes there, he makes this line lighter, this other purer, until a lovely face has grown upon his work. So do you also: cut away all that is excessive, straighten all that is crooked, bring light to all that is overcast, labour to make all one glow of beauty and never cease chiseling your statue, until there shall shine out on you from it the godlike splendour of virtue, until you shall see the perfect goodness surely established in the stainless shrine (I – 6:9).

A guide to union with the One will no longer be necessary when a person has become this complete work where "purity of heart is to will one thing," as the existentialist Kierkegaard once wrote, and nothing external to the innermost soul and intellect makes claim to the essential nature of oneself. Once this stage of growth is reached, Plotinus writes, "you are now become very vision: now call up all your confidence, strike forward yet a step – you need a guide no longer – strain, and see."

The eyes cannot see the sun unless they first become sunlike. The Soul cannot have a clear vision of the "First Beauty" unless it is itself beautiful, too.

---

*Endnotes*

[1] Thomas Merton, *Seven Story Mountain* (New York: Harcourt, 1948), p. 472.
[2] Merton, *The New Man* (New York: Noonday Press, 1961), p. 56.

# 6

# Free Will
# and the One

*Further we must remember what has been already said, that where there is true being, where things have been brought to reality by that Principle – and this is true of whatsoever has determined condition within the order of sense – all that is reality is brought about in virtue of something emanating from the divine* (VI – 8:14).

Is one free to act as one so chooses or is the will of a person somehow enslaved, or at least influenced, by outside forces? In the final analysis, Plotinus leaves no room for speculation regarding this question and uses the opportunity to exalt his idea of the nature of the One and the *Nous*, while bringing low the idea of the free will of the Soul which does not travel the way of enlightenment. For him, freedom and free will are inextricably intertwined with the nature and character of the Supreme Being.

In this chapter we will examine the *Eight Tractate* of the *Sixth Ennead* "On Free Will and the Will of the One," and the intimate connections Plotinus forges between these traditionally opposed concepts. His thesis is clear:

> …the Soul becomes free when it moves, through Intellectual-Principle, towards The Good; what it does in that spirit is its free act; Intellectual-Principle is free in its own right. That principle of Good is the sole object of desire and the source of self-disposal to the rest, to soul when it fully attains, to Intellectual-Principle by connate possession (VI – 8:7).

## Violence to the *Nous*

Does the freedom of the One compare to the freedom of the individual? Or they one and the same? Plotinus argues that it is difficult to conceive of the "free will" of people in terms of the freedom of the One without doing violence to the conception of the *Nous*. He writes:

> It is rash thinking drawn from another order that imagines a First Principle to be chance-made, controlled by a manner of being imposed from without, void therefore of freedom or self-disposal, acting or refraining under compulsion. Such a statement is untrue to its subject and introduces much difficulty; it utterly annuls the principle of freewill with the very conception of our own voluntary action, so that there is no longer any sense in discussion upon these terms, empty names for the non-existent (VI – 8:7).

Whoever reaches this conclusion through such rash thinking, Plotinus says, must be inclined to admit that not only is free act by the will not possible, the words "free" and "will" themselves are meaningless.

He does admit, however, that although conceptually we can begin to speak of freedom in terms of the Tripartite division of reality, this discussion will involve painstaking analysis of an object subject to something outside of itself and an object which is subject (bound) to nothing but its own self. Such an analysis cannot be expected to grasp all of this reality outside of us which itself is our source. If this were possible, we should never need to ask the question concerning free will.

## Man's Freedom

What do we mean when we speak of freedom in ourselves? Plotinus writes:

> Moving as we do amid adverse fortunes, compulsions, violent assaults of passion crushing the soul, feeling ourselves mastered by these experiences, playing slave to them, going where they lead, we have been brought by all this to doubt whether we are anything at all and dispose of ourselves in any particular (VI – 8:1).

We think a free act we freely perform, says Plotinus, believing that "everything will be voluntary that is produced under no compulsion and with knowledge; our free act is what we are masters to perform." In our vanity, we believe we are free to experience freedom and the security it offers.

For example, consider a man who considers himself free to murder, Plotinus asks of us. Such an act will not be voluntary if in the victim he has failed to recognie his own father. Perhaps, however, even this sort of ignorance is not compatible with real freedom: for the knowledge necessary to a voluntary act cannot be limited to certain particulars but must cover the entire field.

Why, for example, should killing be involuntary in the failure to recognize a father and not so in the failure to recognize the wickedness of murder? If because the killer ought to have learned, still ignorance of the duty of learning and the cause of that ignorance remain alike involuntary (VI – 8:1).

But can we place the freedom of action we ascribe to ourselves in the reality of our everyday world? Is it to be located in our various impulses or desires, Plotinus asks, "as when we act or omit in lust or rage or upon some calculation of advantage accompanied by desire?"

> We may be reminded that the Living Form and the soul know what they do. But, if this is knowledge by perception, it does not help towards the freedom of the act; perception gives awareness, not mastery: if true knowing is meant, either this is the knowing of something happening - once more awareness - with the motive-force still to seek, or the reasoning and knowledge have acted to quell the appetite; then we have to ask to what this repression is to be referred and where it has taken place (VI – 8:2).

The question concerns not the motivation for acting, but the mind behind the motivation which conceives of the act and convinces the body to follow. Plotinus calls this the "mental process set(ting) up an opposing desire" and if this is the case free act depends on the workings of the mind (its content and source) and the exploration of act in and of itself has only just begun.

## The Gods and Freedom

What conclusion does Plotinus offer regarding the gods' freedom?

Four steps have been considered up to this point regarding the possibility of freedom. First, self-disposal explains the will and, second, the will requires reasoning. Third, right reasoning is necessary for true freedom of the will and, fourth, right reasoning, therefore, requires proper knowledge. Unfortunately, Plotinus is keenly aware, there are things to be considered which may well be out of the control of the herd-mentality those of us in the "un"-enlightened mass of humanity possess; things such as "fancy."

## Fancy

Plotinus says that regardless of how "sound opinion and act may be they do not yield true freedom when the adoption of the right course is the result of hazard or of some presentment from the fancy with no knowledge of the foundations of that rightness (VI – 8:3)." What role does "fancy," as Plotinus calls it, play in the journey toward right reason and proper knowledge?

Fancy is the body confronting its desires. Whether it is hungry, angry, lonely or tired, it struggles to meet its needs at the cost of losing sight of its goal or movement toward spiritual unity with the One. Plotinus writes:

> We refuse to range under the principle of freedom those whose conduct is directed by such fancy: the baser sort, mainly so guided, cannot be credited with self-disposal or voluntary act. Self-disposal, belongs to those who, through the activities of the Intellectual-Principle, live above the states of the body (VI – 8:3).

There is a dual meaning to the dilemma of fancy which Plotinus would also have us be aware of. It is not just the raw desires of the stomach in need of food or the muscle in need of rest but encompasses the range of encumberance to include mental and spiritual laziness, too. Fancy includes not only the gluttonous but the vain, not only the sluggard but the proverbial fool.

When we find ourselves in a lower, pitiful state our baser side, this thing called fancy, has gotten the best of us, Plotinus says:

> ...by desire or rage or some evil image: the misnamed reasoning that takes up with the false, in reality fancy, has not stayed for the judgement of the Reasoning-Principle: we have acted at the call of

the less worthy, just as in matters of the sense-sphere we sometimes see falsely because we credit only the lower perception, that of the Complement, without applying the tests of the Reasoning-Faculty (I – 1:9).

Freedom rings from the exercise of the *Nous* emanating its desires to the Soul and the Soul, in turn, beckoning the body to follow. These desires, Plotinus says, "are formed in the exercise of the Intellectual act [and] cannot be classed as involuntary."

The gods that live by the principles of the *Nous* and in its realm - desire conformity to it - possess freedom.

## Constraint or Compulsion?

Can constraint, the turning away from diversion, take place when the body is weighted down by its own concerns and there is no compulsion to obey an external influence?

Effort is free once it is towards a fully recognised good; the involuntary is motion away from a good and towards the enforced, towards something not recognised as a good; servitude lies in being powerless to move towards one's good, being debarred from the preferred path in a menial obedience (VI – 8:4).

Plotinus' definition of slavery for the body which attaches itself to the Soul in order to pull it down to earth, is not the hurt and guilt incurred from such action, but from having to swallow the pride in order to yield its kingdom in favor of another body's good, or the good of the One.

The One does not involve "action according to nature," for it cannot have such a duality of master and mastered in a nature which is undivided principle, no differentiation between being and act. Plotinus says:

Where act is performed neither because of another nor at another's will, there surely is freedom. Freedom may of course be an inappropriate term: there is something greater here: it is self-disposal in the sense, only, that there is no disposal by the extern, no outside master over the act (VI – 8:4).

Act and essence must be free. Plotinus says:

No doubt Intellectual-Principle itself is to be referred to a yet higher; but this higher is not extern to it; Intellectual-Principle is within the Good; possessing its own good in virtue of that indwelling, much more will it possess freedom and self-disposal which are sought only for the sake of the good (VI -8:4).

The act of the *Nous* and the One, or the Good are co-equal and such act is self-centered in terms of the greatest good for all things, itself being this greatest good.

## Freedom and the Will

Plotinus asks the question in another way. How is there freedom of the will, when free action is produced – and suppressed by – the will?

The *Nous* and Virtue are sovereign, according to him but only the *Nous* is "self-confined" or truly free, whereas Virtue in its attempt to instruct the Soul is entangled in the Soul's misdemeanor and cannot experience the true freedom it desires, although when it is so negatively influenced, Virtue may "watch still for its sovereignty calling these also to judgement (VI -8:6)."

Virtue, according to Plotinus, does not follow upon occurrences as a saver of the emperilled. It sacrifices - for the highest good - a person at its discretion and may decree the jettison of life, means, children and country. Virtue looks to its own high aim and not to the safeguarding of anything lower and is a mode of the *Nous*, not involving any of the emotions or passions controlled by its reasonings or the body.

Freedom of act (self-disposal) is not tied to the human "doing" but to the human "being," "not to the external thing done but to the inner activity" to the *Nous* and "to virtue's own vision," according to Plotinus.

Ultimately, only the unembodied is the free:

...to this our self-disposal is to be referred; herein lies our will which remains free and self-disposing in spite of any orders which it may necessarily utter to meet the external. All then that issues from will and is the effect of will is our free action...(VI – 8:6).

All that exists outside of the flesh is truly free to will and act in freedom.

The contemplating *Nous*, the First or Highest is self-disposal to the point that its operation is utterly independent. It turns wholly upon itself, is in its very action itself, is at rest in its good and, finally, is without need. It is complete and may be said to live to its will.

According to Plotinus, the contemplating *Nous* is the Will set free. It is called will because it expresses the *Nous* in the willing-phase - what we know as will imitates this operation taking place within the *Nous*. Will strives towards the good which the act of the *Nous* realizes. What will seeks is that good whose attainment makes will identical with the *Nous*.

## Freedom from Necessity

For Plotinus, the ability to choose A over B, for example, to either put aside *On Plotinus* and go out for a jog or to continue reading it and have another snack, is not the measure of true freedom in the individual. Choice and freedom are not co-equal. Instead, true freedom for the person in the above scenario would be the ability to go against the cravings of the body and soul, the necessity these cravings involve. True freedom not to snack if snacking is an inescapable passion or not to run if running is an escape from reality which allows her respite from a childhood trauma she avoids facing up to.

Hesitation, for Plotinus, is the death knell for the Soul intent on escaping the struggle between good and evil, between the purified Soul and the Soul governed by impurity and multiplicity. The Soul that hesitates before the choice of going against the passions is not free, is not in communion with the One. What is in his view true communion with the One is the girl's desire to change and to realize change is necessary. Quite often this desire is the only thing the Soul searching for union with the One can recognize as pure within itself, as the potential power of awakening yet to be realized.

Questions remain, however, for the reader of Plotinus' philosophy. These are crucial questions and must be asked without expecting clear answers forthcoming. For example, just how corrupted are a person's desires, how much can I help myself toward communion with the One, or, along the same line, how much can I expect the One to assist me in this daunting task? These, too, remain - even among the technological and medical advances of modern science - the unanswered questions of the moral philosopher, the psychologist, and the theologian who pursue an idealism beyond empirical certainty.

## On Freedom in the Supreme

In his *Sixth Ennead*, Plotinus presents a poetic tribute towards an understanding of how the One is and, consequently, appropriates true freedom of being. He writes:

> Lovable, very love, the Supreme is also self-love in that He is lovely no otherwise than from Himself and in Himself. Self-presence can hold only in the identity of associated with associating; since, in the Supreme, associated and associating are one, seeker and sought one - the sought serving as Hypostasis and substrate of the seeker - once more God's being and his seeking are identical: once more, then, the Supreme is the self-producing, sovereign of Himself, not happening to be as some extern willed but existing as He wills it (VI – 8:15).

Because the Supreme does not "absorb anything nor [does] anything absorb Him," writes Plotinus, he remains unique, untouched, and outside of all events. If we were are able to extend this characteristic of the One to ourselves and to conceive of our own nature as remaining unaffected by all the chaos and uncertainty of events which constantly occur around us, we would begin to understand what it is like to experience complete freedom within our own being.

> ...by this new state alone we acquire self-disposal and free act, the freedom of that light which belongs to the order of the good and is good in actuality, greater than anything Intellectual-Principle has to give, an actuality whose advantage over Intellection is no adventitious superiority (VI- 8:15).

To reach this place and to become "This alone," Plotinus writes, would mean that we would be beyond free - if one can imagine such a state - and more self-disposed to experience such a state of release. To reach this place would also precipitate a severance from the wiles of chance, hazard and happenstance, a place where "we are become veritable Life," and have "entered into That which contains no alloy but is purely itself?"

Alas, per chance we dream, aware that the human "being" distracted from such a place is inadequate for the task at hand, whereas the Supreme in isolation is still what it is – truly free.

# 7

# On Evil, Providence and Gnosticism

In spite of the brevity of Plotinus' literary output, over two-fifths of it was produced in the period 263-268, when Porphyry was studying with Plotinus. Perhaps Porphyry's presence worked as a powerful stimulus. A considerable part of the output of this period is devoted to polemics with other schools, notably against Gnosticism.

## Polemic against Gnosticism

Of all the polemics of Plotinus, the most significant is the one against Gnosticism. One could say that when facing Gnostic pessimism point-blank, Plotinus overcompensates for the pessimistic and Gnostic strand present in himself and responds with an almost unlimited optimism.

The fundamental mood underlying Gnosticism is alienation from a hostile world, and Gnosticism undertakes to explain this mood and to open the road to escape from the world. The explanation is in the form of a history of the origin of the visible cosmos; according to Gnosticism, this cosmos is the result of the activity of an evil god sometimes identified with the Creator-God of the Old Testament or with Plato's divine artisan. This evil god is only the last in a succession of beings. The manner in which this succession takes place consists in a number of voluntary acts by which divinities of an ever lower order originate.

The relation between these deities is often personal, based on such traits as curiosity, oblivion, daring, and ambition. Man, as he exists in this evil world, contains in himself a spark of what was his original, divine substance, now imprisoned in his body owing to the scheming of the evil god. At a certain moment a messenger-savior in some way breaks the power of the evil god and makes it possible for those who hear the whole story (acquire gnosis) to regain their original standing and free themselves from the tyranny of the evil god.

In his "Summary" of the *Ninth Tractate* of the *Second Ennead*, MacKenna cuts to the heart of Plotinus' disdain for Gnostic philosophy:

> What he particularly dislikes about them is their irreverence for the Greek philosophical tradition, their undisciplined multiplication of spiritual entities and use of jargon, and their claim to be a uniquely privileged order of beings. Their hatred of the material universe actually leads him to take a particularly positive attitude to it here (108).

Plotinus treats Gnosticism as a strictly philosophic system. He simply compares its doctrines with his own and with those of Plato; its salvationary aspects are of little interest to him:

> And, what are we to think of the new forms of being they introduce – their 'Exiles' and 'Impressions' and 'Repentings'? If all comes to states of the Soul – 'Repentence' when it has undergone a change of purpose; 'Impressions' when it contemplates not the Authentic Existences but their simulacra – there is nothing here but a jargon invented to make a case for their school: all this terminology is piled up only to conceal their debt to the ancient Greek philosophy which taught, clearly and without bombast, the ascent from the cave and the gradual advance of souls to a truer and truer vision (II – 9:6)

Plotinus' reference to the "ascent from the cave" at this point comes both to offer his reverence for the clarity Plato is reknowned for and to establish the Gnostic tendency to muddy the waters and to establish a philosophy from "novelties...picked up outside the truth."

In *Book VII* of his *Republic*, Plato offers his famous allegory of a cave to show how the lack of education in the nature of true reality can be dangerous. As the allegory goes, a long passageway at the cave's mouth leads to its interior where men, who have been chained at their legs and neck since childhood are held captive. In fact, they are chained in such a way (blinders and all) that they cannot turn their heads and must look directly ahead at the back of the cave wall.

A fire burns at a higher elevation somewhere behind them and there is a raised wall between the prisoners and the fire and puppeteers crouch behind this wall moving their puppets above the raised wall so that the shadows from the puppets are cast on the cave wall the prisoners stare at. They have always and only seen these shadows all these years. This is the only reality they know.

At some point in the madness, however, one of the prisoners is freed from his chains, stands up and turns around, and even though the light is blinding, he walks toward it. He is disoriented, confused, and he has no idea what all these puppeteers are all about. But Plato doesn't give him enough time to examine the evidence before he is seized upon and dragged by force out of the cave into direct sunlight.

It is now about "habituation" for the prisoner. In time he will surely see the sun rise and set and come to understand there is such a thing as day and night beyond the perpetual darkness of cave-dwelling. When he becomes enlightened in this way, surely he will want to rush back into the cave and free his fellow prisoners, right? But will they believe him, or will they think he has lost his mind and is spreading false hope born of illusion?

Plato's point is that there is already this kind of escape to reason in the soul of every person but not every person will believe the truth when it is put before them. As is the case with Gnosticism, so Plotinus argues, they have merely adulterated the obvious truth contained in Plato's theories and would rather enjoy the puppet show of shadows in their own self-created cave of darkness.

Specific examples of the Gnostic heresy Plotinus discusses are in the succession of divine beings where he sees only a superfluous multiplication of the three hypostases of his own system and the cosmic drama which results in the creation of the visible cosmos, where he opposes his view of a totally undramatic, unconscious emanation, a product of necessity without arbitrariness and, contradicting even Plato's *Timaeus* (40B-45A), without planning (V - 8:7) and, therefore, entirely blameless. The cosmos, product of the activities of the Soul (or *Nous* or both), Plotinus considers to be beautiful.

Whereas Gnosticism sees the visible universe filled with spirits inimical to man, most outstanding among them being the rulers of the celestial bodies (planets), Plotinus sees in these spirits powers related to man in brotherly fashion. What is true in Gnosticism can, according to him, be found in Plato. The Gnostic objection that Plato did not penetrate the mysteries of the intelligible world Plotinus considers ridiculously presumptuous:

> As a matter of fact the ancient doctrine of the Divine Essences was far the sounder and more instructed, and must be accepted by all not caught in the delusions that beset humanity: it is easy to identify what has been conveyed in these later times from the ancients with incongruous novelties – how for example, where they must set up a contradictory doctrine, they introduce a medley of generation and destruction, how they cavil at the Universe, how they make the Soul blameable for the association with the body, how they revile the Administrator of this All, how they ascribe to the Creator, identified with the Soul, the character and experiences appropriate to partial beings (II – 9:6).

In the end of his polemic, Plotinus narrows the heart of the Gnostic problem of the reality of the world to its false dualistic theories concerning good and evil, or more precisely the body and soul as related to good and evil. He writes that "as long as we have bodies we must inhabit the dwellings prepared for us by our good sister soul (the All-Soul) in her vast power of labourless creation (II – 9:18)."

To understand this according to Plotinus, imagine two people living in a stately house. One of the people hates the house and thinks the architect who designed it got his license in the mail. The other person believes the architect to be cut from the cloth of Frank Lloyd Wright and cherishes the home. The "malcontent" thinks he is smarter than "Mr. Positive" because he knows a bad house when he sees one and is prepared to leave the place at a moment's notice.

The only real problem the malcontent has, Plotinus says, is that he isn't able to "bear with necessity" this soulless stone and timber that comprise his temporary dwelling, and in such a manner as to offer respect to the Architect who will one day offer him a much grander place to live.

## Ecstatic Union

*And since the higher exists, there must be the lower as well. The Universe is a thing of variety, and how could there be an inferior without a superior or a superior without an inferior? We cannot*

63

*complain about the lower in the higher; rather, we must be grateful to the higher for giving something of itself to the lower* (III – 3:7).

As is to be expected, some earlier themes recur in the third period. In fact, one of the essays of the third period contains what is perhaps the most comprehensive presentation of the basic tenets of Plotinus' philosophy. Plotinus proves that there must be a One preceding all multiplicity and that this One must be ineffable. He uses sunlight to explain:

> The entire intellectual order may be figured as a kind of light with the One in repose at its summit as its King: but this manifestation is not cast out from it – that would cause us to postulate another light before the light – but the One shines eternally, resting upon the Intellectual Realm; this, not identical with its source, is yet not severed from it nor of so remote a nature as to be less than Real-Being; it is no blind thing, but is seeing, self-knowing, the primal knower (V – 3:12).

To explain its presence in us and the fact that we know about it although we do not know it, he says that those full of and possessed by the divine also feel that something greater than themselves is present in them, although they cannot say what it is. It is not by knowledge or reason, Plotinus concludes, we are able to grasp the presence, although there is an intuitive awareness of this presence. "We hold it not so as to state it, but so as to be able to speak about it. And we can and do state what it is not, while we are silent as to what it is: we are, in fact, speaking of it in the light of its sequels; unable to state it, we may still possess it (V – 3:14)."

Once more facing the problem of how the One, which is absolutely simple, can be the source of multiplicity, Plotinus is on the verge of admitting that the One is at least potentially many - though it is a potentiality *sui generic,* as the Latin would have it, "alone of its kind" (V - 3:15; VI - 5:9). The same essay contains what is probably the most detailed and impressive description of the upward journey of the soul to reach the goal of ecstatic union, described by the formula "through light light" (V – 3:17; V – 5:4-9).

As advice on how to achieve this union, Plotinus says "strip yourself of everything." Continuing with "light" as the heart of his analogy, the conclusion of the *Third Tractate* is classic ancient prose:

At the moment of touch there is no power whatever to make any affirmation; there is no leisure; reasoning upon the vision is for afterwards. We may know we have had the vision when the Soul has suddenly taken light. This light is from the Supreme and is the Supreme; we may believe in the Presence when, like that other God on the call of a certain man, He comes bringing light: the light is the proof of the advent. Thus, the Soul unlit remains without that vision; lit, it possesses what it sought. And this is the true end set before the Soul, to take the light, to see the Supreme by the Supreme and not by the light of any other principle – to see the Supreme which is also the means to the vision; for that which illumines the Soul is that which it is to see, just as it is by the sun's own light that we see the sun. But how is this to be accomplished? Cut away everything (V – 3:17).

## Theodicy

On the whole, the writings of Plotinus' last period are dominated by two themes. The first concerns theodicy, the origin and justification of evil, and the second asks what man's true self is.

To explain the origin of evil, Plotinus tries to reconcile the view that matter, though void of any quality and actually only deficiency, is still evil in some sense of the word and is the source of all evil:

Matter becomes mistress of what is manifested through it: it corrupts and destroys the incomer, it substitutes its own opposite character and kind, not in the sense of opposing, for example, concrete cold to concrete warmth, but by setting its own formlessness against the Form of heat, shapelessness to shape, excess and defect to the duly ordered (I – 8:8).

Plotinus comes dangerously close to the Gnostic theory that matter imprisons the soul and to a completely dualistic system when he writes that "if body is the cause of Evil, then there is no escape; the cause of Evil is Matter (I – 8:8)."

Or, in the same section he explains that matter exists and Soul exists and they both occupy the same place. "This is the fall of the Soul, this entry into Matter..." he writes, and "thus the cause, at once, of the weakness of Soul and of all its evil is Matter (I – 8:8)."

65

Nevertheless, his optimism is particularly strong in this period; he has high praise for the beauty of the visible cosmos (III – 2:12), and rejects the idea of an evil creator of the cosmos (III – 2:1). His theodicy is a blend of Platonic arguments, drawn especially from Book X of the Laws, and Stoic arguments.

Perfection of the whole demands imperfection of the parts (III – 2:11,17 and III - 3) and the existence of evil (I – 8:8-15). At the same time he minimizes the importance of evil by insisting that it exists only for the wicked one (III – 2:6). Furthermore, he points out that the cosmic order rewards and punishes everybody according to his merits and assigns each one an appropriate place, thus making for a completely harmonious whole (III – 2:4).

Ultimately, his theodicy is based on convictions characteristic of most theodicies - that to designate a particular as evil is to lose sight of the whole, that everything participates in the good as far as it can, and that evil is only absence of the good:

> There is no injustice in a man suffering what belongs to the condition in which he is; nor can we ask to be happy when our actions have not earned us happiness; the good, only are happy; divine beings are happy only because they are good (III – 2:4).

## The Soul and Evil

The idea of Moral Evil, the formidable problem of how the soul, the essence of which is unchangeability, can ever become evil also vexed Plotinus to the end (I – 8:4, 12, 15). In the work of his last period he explains that as the soul at its descent acquires additional parts, evil resides only in them. Thus, the ethical task of man is not so much to separate the soul from the body as it is to separate it from these adventitious parts (I – 1:12).

In this context the problem of who is the subject of punishments in after-life also emerges; Plotinus answers that it is that "composite" soul (I – 1:12). Why we should call soul an entity which is or can become evil, "suffer" punishment, and so on, after Soul has been presented as belonging to the realm of the unchangeable, remains unanswered; so do virtually all questions resulting from the dual character of *Nous* and Soul as metaphysical (transcendental) entities on the one hand and human (immanent) entities on the other.

66

There is almost something providential in the fact that the very last of Plotinus' essays, written at a time when death was approaching him, reasserts that all things participate in the One (the Good) and discusses the question of how to reconcile the two thesis that life is good and yet death no evil, though it deprives us of something good (I – 7:3). The battle between the pessimistic and the optimistic strands of Plotinus continued to the very end of his activity. Optimism ultimately won: Life is good – though not for the wicked one; death is good, because it will permit the soul to live an unhampered life.

## Providence

Closely connected with the problem of theodicy is the problem of providence. Plotinus insists on the all-pervasive character of providence, thus rejecting Aristotle's dichotomy of the universe into a sublunar sphere dominated by necessity and a supralunar world to which providence is restricted. He replaces Aristotle's distinction by the dichotomy of good and wicked men; only the wicked are subject to necessity:

> And that law enjoins that those who have made themselves good shall know the best of life, here and later, the bad the reverse. But the law does not warrant the wicked in expecting that their prayers should bring others to sacrifice themselves for their sakes; or that the gods should lay aside the divine life in order to direct their daily concerns...(III – 2:9).

Certainly, too, The One is not subject to division, which is the primeval cause of wickedness. The One knows no spatial distinction, and has no division in itself. Even its parts have no incompleteness among them and the individual part is not served from the entire.

"In this nature inheres all life and all intellect," writes Plotinus, "a life living and having intellection as one act within a unity: every part that it gives forth is a whole; all its content is its very own, for there is no separation of thing from thing, no part standing in isolated existence estranged from the rest, and therefore nowhere is there any wronging of any other, even among contraries (III – 2:1)."

But this providence is entirely impersonal and actually coincides with the order of the universe:

No: all turns on the necessary completeness of Act; we cannot think anything belonging to God to be other than a whole and all and therefore in anything of God's that in all must be contained...(VI – 7:1).

In the *Third Ennead*, the *Second* and *Third Tractate(s)* contain Plotinus' *First* and *Second Treatise(s)* on *Providence*. These are designed to uphold or defend both the existence and goodness of divine Providence against the challenge of the problem of evil and against particular attacks on the nature and character of Providence opponents such as the Epicureans put forth.

# 8

# Beauty and Self-Knowledge

*Therefore, first let each become godlike and each beautiful who cares to see God and Beauty* (I – 6:9)

## On Beauty

In the *Sixth Tractate* of the *First Ennead*, Plotinus unfolds his fascination with the idea of beauty. His encounter with beauty is not only of the perceptual sort where "a rose is a rose," but also an immaterial sort where there is such a thing as "intellectual" beauty and the shining forth of the beauty of the One.

This *Tractate* is one of the earliest recorded works of Plotinus and is noted for its tedious exposition of his aesthetics. The work is said to be based on the speeches of Diotima recorded in Plato's *Symposium*. A priestess and prophetess she, according to the *Symposium* itself, is said to have opened Socrates' eyes to the true mysteries of Eros.

The question of beauty is prepared for its answer by Plotinus with this quote itself replete with questions:

> What then is it that gives comeliness to material forms and draws the ear to the sweetness perceived in sounds, and what is the secret of beauty there is in all that derives from Soul? Is there One Principle from which all take their grace, or is there a beauty peculiar to the embodied and another for the bodiless? Finally, one or many, what would such a Principle be (I – 1:1)

The order which Plotinus follows is: first, to criticize the Stoic theory of beauty; secondly, to develop his own idea of beauty; thirdly, to examine the idea of beauty as it applies to the Soul; fourthly, a discussion of the beauty of the One and the goal of striving for unity with this beauty.

## *Against the Stoics*

Against the Stoics, Plotinus argues that the individual parts of a whole are not in themselves beautiful but are simply sharing in the beauty provided by the whole, but at the same time not one of the parts could be ugly for if it were the whole could not be beautiful. This appears on the surface to be circular reasoning, but once it is understood that the Stoic teaching was that something of beauty could contain elements of "non-beauty," that the two might co-exist, Plotinus' reasoning becomes clear, although it isn't necessarily convincing.

Just as the cumulative gathering of virtues are all characteristic of the beautiful Soul, Plotinus argues, all things beautiful whether material or immaterial possess the symmetry of being accordant with each other in part and in whole.

## *Plontinus' Theory of Beauty*

The theory that bestows beauty on material things for Plotinus is "something that is perceived at first glance, something which the Soul names as from an ancient knowledge and, recognizing, welcomes it, enters into unison with it (I – 6:2)." The Soul which "falls in with the Ugly" will instantly shrink within itself, deny beauty, turn away from it, and, ultimately, resent it.

Plotinus discusses his theory of beauty in terms of Forms and this in terms of the Ideal-Form. Shapeless form, he writes, that remains outside of Reason and Idea, outside of the Divine-Thought, is ugly solely because of its exclusion from unity with the beauty emanating from the Divine. This is the Absolute Ugly for him, the thing which has not been given over to Reason, unyielding to the Ideal-Form which possesses unity in its matter.

Unity brings forth beauty and "beauty enthrones itself, giving itself to the parts as to the sum," Plotinus writes. An example is that of the beauty of a house with all of its individual parts assembled by the expert craftsman, right down to the single beautiful stone which when placed with many others of its kind form the walls of this house.

The example has further use as well, for Plotinus would have us imagine the craftsman standing before the home he has just created:

> On what principle does the architect, when he finds the home standing before him correspondent with his inner ideal of a house,

pronounce it beautiful? Is it not that the house before him, the stones apart, is the inner idea stamped upon the mass of exterior matter, , the indivisible exhibited in diversity (I – 6:3).

What does he see in his creation with the perceptive faculties he possesses? He considers the Ideal-Form which is the whole of the house built brick by brick from its parts and he witnesses "further stamped upon the common shape" of the parts the "excellent above the common." The house stands before him in likeness to the One, gathering into unity what remains fragmentary, catching it up and carrying it into unity. This house is "no longer a thing of its parts, and presents it to the Ideal-Principle as something concordant and congenial, a natural friend."

The joy experienced for the craftsman standing before his handiwork, Plotinus writes, "is like that of a good man who discerns in youth the early signs of a virtue consonant with the achieved perfection within his own soul (I – 6:3)."

## *Beauty in the Soul*

What is Plotinus idea of beauty as it applies to the Soul? Is the beauty of the Soul comparable to that of the material body? To properly answer these questions, he asks us to imagine people who are born blind:

> As it is not for those to speak of the graceful forms of the material world who have never seen them or known their grace – men born blind, let us suppose – in the same way those must by silent upon the beauty of noble conduct and of learning and all that order who have never cared for such things, nor may those tell of the splendour of virtue who have never known the face of Justice and of Moral-Wisdom beautiful beyond the beauty of Evening and of Dawn (I – 6:4).

Beauty of the Soul is not really properly understood unless it is discussed by those who themselves have received an awareness of this other-wordly Beauty from outside their own reasoning capabilities.

The contrary to such beauty, what Plotinus calls "the ugliness of Soul" is a deplorable and pitiful state indeed. "It is no longer a clean activity or a clean sensation, but commands only a life smouldering dully under the crust of evil," Plotinus writes, and "sunk in manifold death, it no longer sees what a Soul should see, may no longer rest in its own being," and it is "dragged ever as it is towards the outer, the lower, the dark (I – 6:5)?"

So, as the Soul becomes ugly by "something foisted upon it" or "by sinking itself into the alien," with a descent into the body and the carnal, so it is restored to beauty through purification of the body which calls for great Courage, Wisdom, and Magnanimity, not to forget an insatiable appetite for moral discipline and every virtue.

In the end, the Soul that finds cleansing through this difficult path will be wholly free of body and released into the realm of "that divine order from which the wellspring of Beauty rises and all the race of Beauty (I – 6:6)."

## Beauty and the One

The Soul which is cleansed of the Absolute Ugly of Plotinus to become a beautiful thing is also becoming "like to God," and it is from the One that all Beauty is derived as well as the Good that exists in all beings. He makes an all-encompassing statement of the comparison of Beauty and Ugliness with unity and disunity and with the One and Multiplicitiy:

> We may even say that Beauty is the Authentic-Existents and Ugliness is the Principle contrary to Existence: and the Ugly is also the primal evil; therefore its contrary is at once good and beautiful, or is Good and Beauty: and hence the one method will discover to us the Beauty-Good and the Ugliness-Evil (I – 6:6).

This Beauty, this Authentic-Existents, which is also the Good, is also the First, Plotinus writes. Directly emanating from the First is the *Nous* which is actually the manifestation of Beauty and through the *Nous* the Soul is made beautiful. The progression from the One, through the *Nous*, and settling at last in the Soul possessing unity with the One is once again made circumspect in his grammar of ascent and descent.

This ascent toward true Beauty which must follow the descent into Ugliness begins with the action of self-questioning. One must ask oneself how is it possible to know the Soul's loveliness? Plotinus' answer to this question comprises some of his best writing and a lays down a gauntlet of challenge to the Soul in search of loveliness:

> Withdraw into yourself and look. And if you do not find yourself beautiful yet, act as does the creator of a statue that is to be made beautiful: he cuts away here, he smoothes there, he makes this line lighter, this other purer, until a lovely face has grown upon his work. So do you also: cut away all that is excessive, straighten all that is crooked, bring light to all that is overcast, labour to make all one glow of beauty and never cease chiseling your statue, until there shall shine out on you form it the godlike splendour of virtue, until you shall see the perfect goodness surely established in the stainless shrine (I – 6:9).

## Know Thy Self

*There is the man, too, that lives partly in the one allegiance and partly in the other; he is a blend of the good that is himself with the evil that is alien ( VI – 4:16).*

Inscribed on the temple Delphi the Greek oracle - "Know Thyself" major theme in the last period of Plotinus' writings considers this divine command. Plotinus' version of the statement might be "Know Thy 'True' Self," and this in order to experience true well-being and happiness.

A person's true self is difficult to place in the philosophy of Plotinus, however, and for the quandary already encountered, that of metaphysical entities such as the One and the *Nous* remaining transcendent while continuing to commune with the levels of the Soul where the body and matter exist.

> It would be absurd to think that happiness begins and ends with the living-body: happiness is the possession of the good life: it is centered therefore in Soul, is an Act of the Soul – and not of all the Soul at that: for it certainly is not characteristic of the vegetative soul, the soul of growth; that would at once connect it with the body (I – 4:14).

A solution Plotinus offers regarding the present dilemma is to posit the theory that a person's real self is found in the realm of the

*Nous*, if a person is able to discover the reality of the *Nous*. At the same time, ironically, the realm of the *Nous* is closer to the person than she would know. There must be a way, he thinks, to be convinced that one has attained this "power of an ever-fresh infinity, a principle unfailing, inexhaustible, at no point giving out, brimming over with its own vitality." He writes:

> In that you have entered into the All, no longer content with the part; you cease to think of yourself as under limit but, laying all such determination aside, you become an All. No doubt you were always that, but there has been an addition and by that addition you are diminished; for the addition was not from the realm of Being – you can add nothing to Being – but from non-Being. It is not by some admixture of non-Being that one becomes an entire, but by putting non-Being away (I – 4:9).

The unconscious plays a decisive role in the system of Plotinus, He writes that "it may perhaps be urged that sensation and consciousness are essential to wisdom and that happiness is only wisdom brought to act (I - 4:9)."

All this ties in with the idea that self-knowledge occurs only when the subject, the act, and the object of knowledge coincide – which takes place only on the level of the *Nous* – whereas neither a person as a whole nor the Soul can possess full self-knowledge:

> Because we have allotted to the Soul the function of dealing – in thought and in multiform action – with the external, and we hold that observation of self and the content of self must belong to the Intellectual-Principle.

According to Plotinus, if a person says, 'Still; what precludes the reasoning Soul from observing its own content by some special faculty?' this person "is no longer positing a principle of understanding or of reasoning but, simply, bringing in the Intellectual-Principle unalloyed (V – 3:3)."

The One is, of course, is above any kind of self-knowledge and it has no need for what Plotinus deems "minute self-handling" because "it has nothing to learn by an intellective act; it is in full possession of its being before Intellect exists."

Knowledge implies desire, for it is, so to speak, discovery crowning a search; the utterly undifferentiated remains self-centred and makes no inquiry about the self: anything capable of analyzing its content must be a manifold (V – 3:10-13).

The thesis that only the *Nous* is a person's true self (if and when he makes full use of it) serves also as a basis for a discussion of the problem of a person's happiness. If by "person" we mean the composite of body and soul, a person cannot experience happiness, nor can one if one is body alone.

However, if by "person" we mean the true self, it is obvious that happiness consists in the exercise of the *Nous* - that is, in contemplation. But as the activity of the *Nous* is uninterrupted (here in the argument Plotinus switches from the *Nous* as immanent to transcendent *Nous*; see I - 1:13) a person is actually always happy, although one may remain unconscious of it.

# 9
# Metaphysical Difficulties

*Everyone has warned me not to tell you what I am going to tell you...They all say 'The ordinary reader does not want Theology; give him plain, practical religion.' I have rejected their advice. I do not think the ordinary reader is such a fool. Theology means 'the science of God' and I think any man who wants to think about God at all would like to have the clearest and most accurate ideas about Him which are available. You are not children; why should you be treated like children?*

---C.S. Lewis[1]

There is no doubt Plotinus would agree with theologian Lewis' quote above wholeheartedly, having dedicated most of his lifetime study of philosophy and theology to a clarification of what is today known as "perfect being" theology. It is in the Second Period of his life Plotinus engages difficulties inherent in this philosophy. These difficulties in the areas of ethics, sensation, matter and relationships between the hypostases will be discussed in the next two chapters.

## The One

Is the One of Plotinus a necessary being or a free one (*ens necessarium* or *ens liberum*)? Must God exist or has he freely chosen to exist?

To quote Lewis again:

Almost certainly God is not in Time. His life does not consist in moments following one another...If a million people are praying to Him tonight at ten-thirty, He need not listen to them all in that one little snippet which we call ten-thirty. Ten-thirty – and every other moment from the beginning of the world – is always the present for Him. If you like to put it that way, He has all eternity in which to listen to the split second of prayer put up by a pilot as his plane crashes in flames...(142).

In the Eastern tradition, Vivekananda attempts to capture the essence of God in a poem:

He who is in you and outside of you
Who works through all hands
Who walks on his feet
Him worship and break all other idols
In whom is neither past life
Nor future birth nor death
In whom we have always been
And always shall be one...[2]

In what is perhaps his most profound theological discussion, Plotinus tries to establish the concept of the One as Lord of itself and thus not having to serve even itself, so that in the One freedom and necessity coincide. He navigates this difficulty by explaining God as pure Act:

The answer is that we utterly must not speak of Him as made but sheerly as maker; the making must be taken as absolved from all else; no new existence is established; the Act here is not directed to an achievement but is God Himself unalloyed: here is no duality but without Essence; on the contrary the Activity is the very reality (VI – 8:20).

Reality without activity is not reality at all, Plotinus says, and to suppose the One as having Essence without that Essence being synonymous with Act is to suppose nothing at all. Actually, taking the analogy one step further, Act is a more perfect thing than even Essence.

"By acting He is at once Activity," says Plotinus, "and there is no question of 'existing before coming into existence'; when He acted He was not in some state that could be described as 'before existing'. He was already existent entirely (VI – 8:20)."

Activity not under the category of Essence is pure freedom, or is completely free, Plotinus concludes that "God's selfhood, then, is of his own Act. If his being has to be ensured by something else, He is no longer the self-existent First: if it be true pure unity (VI – 8:20)."

For the most part, Judeo-Christian theology would agree with Plotinus. The God of the Bible is act in being. He is not static or immobile but acts to create and interacts with His creation.

The finite mind meets with great difficulty in attempting to grasp the idea that a Supreme Being could be the intersection, or the unity of both potentiality and actuality and in this union represent a dynamic and unceasing becoming. Most theologians would say without qualification, however, that God is forever and has always been an eternal being freely relating to himself, his creation and to his creatures. All possibility realized in the world is already realized in the mind of God and it is God who unceasingly gives these possibilities reality in the temporal world.

For the Judeo-Christian theologian as for Plotinus, there is communion with God with himself even before he acts to create and commune with the world and is very being is in his very action, even though one should be careful not to say that he is obliged to act in a given way at a given time.

There are, however, certain difficulties inherent in Plotinus' doctrine of extreme transcendence challenged by traditional Christian theology. The most recurrent criticism addresses Plotinus' pantheistic notions inherent in the union of the three hypostasis, or more precisely, the relation of the One to the many previously encountered.

At the very least, the idea of emanation brings to question the divine transcendence. The very act of creation precludes transcendence and an understanding of a distinction and 'space' between creator and creation. If this space were not carved out the world would be self-creating. How to imagine such a thing? Of course, equally daunting, is trying to imagine a Creator who himself is uncreated.

The question is whether Plotinus' doctrine of emanation leaves sufficient space between transcendence and immanence. My explanation of the Godhead of Plotinus' in Chapter Two does offer a possible explanation towards the above criticism - the idea that the One is simply the transcendent aspect of the Godhead and not itself an entity that actually conceives of or creates space between the *Nous* and the Soul.

## *Nous* and Soul

The *Nous*, Plotinus reiterates contains within itself ideas: "…it must know unceasingly and never forget…(V - 5:1)." It contains multiplicity, in spite of being one in unity: "...in virtue of their infinite nature their unity is a multiplicity, many in one and one over many, a unit-plurality (VI – 5:6)." Plotinus attempts to explain how souls can have plurality and be part of the unity of the World-Soul, too:

> The Beings of the Intellectual are thus a plurality of firsts and seconds and thirds attached like one sphere to one centre, not separated by interval but mutually present; where, therefore, the Intellectual tertiaries are present the secondaries and firsts are present too (VI – 5:4).

Both *Nous* and Soul are present in the sensible world and present in what is extended, although they themselves are not extended. They are also omnipresent and ubiquitous in what is extended and are of a differentiated unity, which is to say that there is a non-contradictory character of "one" and "many."

## Intelligence, Soul, Change

Plotinus' theory in which he holds the *Nous* and the Soul as both metaphysical and present in man (both transcendent and immanent) is difficult to understand. Ideas regarding the *Nous* and the Soul seem to change, whereas in the realm beyond reason they supposedly remain unchanged. How is this so?

Plotinus struggles with these difficulties in many ways during the Second Period. On the one hand, the human soul is separated from the processes of the senses - the soul observes these processes without being affected by them. Or, he might say, he insists that it is not the soul but a trace of it engaged in activities. On the other hand, Plotinus disallows memory to the *Nous* and the Soul entirely.

As to sensing, he distinguishes two kinds, one serving such practical purposes as self-preservation, the other purely theoretical; it is only the theoretical kind which he ascribes to metaphysical entities, the implication obviously being that this kind of sensation does not cause any change in the perceiver.

Perhaps the most striking example of the real effects of the Soul's falling away from the *Nous* (despite everything said by Plotinus to minimize these effects) is that the cosmic soul, as it falls away, engenders time because of an inability to contemplate the totality of the *Nous* simultaneously (III - 7:11).

Having discussed problems inherent to the One, the *Nous* and the Soul, the subjects of ethics, memory and sensation, and matter are examined.

## Ethics

In Plotinus' theory of emanation the progress is from God to the world; Plotinus' moral philosophy is the reverse process or the return to God. Man is able to make this return by means of purification from matter (catharsis). Such a purification is marked by three states: practical, contemplative and ecstatic. Accordingly, there are three grades of virtue.

The *Ethical* virtues are practical and are concerned with and attached to the world. They are not evil in themselves, but there is always the danger that they might oppose and rule the higher virtues in man.

The *Dianoetic* virtues, the second grade of catharsis or purification is marked by the function of contemplative virtues ("dianoetic" being from the Greek: "I know throughout"). Plotinus divides these into aesthetic and rational virtues. Aesthetic virtues separate intelligibles from matter and contemplates them as they exist in the world soul. Rational virtues contemplate as true intelligible ideas separated from matter.

The *Ecstatic* virtues, unlike the ethical and dianoetic virtues cannot lead us to the One. This can be done only through ecstasy, the supreme degree of virtue. In the state of ecstasy man remains passive and unconscious of everything except his union with the One.

The difficulties created for the explanation of the cognitive aspects of man's mental life without the assumption of a real change (possibility) of the soul return with even greater significance in the field of ethics. If there is no actual fall of the soul and if no deterioration of its nature has taken place as the result of incarnation, why is purifying the soul necessary? The answer, according to Plotinus, is that the "affective phase of the Soul" (the Soul working toward purity) must seek separation from external forces. He writes:

> In the particular case of the affective phase of the Soul, purification is its awakening from the baseless visions which beset it, the refusal to see them; its separation consists in limiting its descent towards the lower and accepting no picture thence, and of

course in the banning of all that it ignores when the pneuma (finer-body or spirit) on which it is poised is not turbid from gluttony and surfeit of impure flesh, but is a vehicle so slender that the Soul may ride upon it in tranquility (III – 6:6).

The concept of purification plays a central role in the ethics of Plotinus; he even describes the perfections - wisdom, self-control, justice, courage - as purifications. Plotinus tries to help himself by a metaphor. The soul is merely covered with mud, which, however, has never penetrated it. According to another explanation, what the soul has acquired because of its fall is nothingness, and all it has to do, therefore, is to get rid of nothing.

Plotinus says that "it is not by some admixture of non-Being that one becomes an entire, but by putting non-Being away. By the lessening of the alien in you, you increase (VI – 5:12)." If you attempt to put this "alien" aside, to rid yourself of it, you will discover unity, but if you continue to take up communion with the alien, unity will evade you. It is not unity, however, that will come and find you and release you from it, but it is you, yourself, must recognize the responsibility that is before you. "...turn though you may, you have not severed yourself; it is there; you are not in some far region: still there before it, you have faced to its contrary," so Plotinus believes (VI – 5:12).

## Memory and Sensation

The insistence that memory and sensation, in their ordinary senses, are absent from the realm of the *Nous* and even from that of the celestial sphere Plotinus explains with his theory that the universe is one animated organism. The sympathy existing among parts of one organism make memory and sensation superfluous, since the mutual affection need not be perceived.

This leads to characteristic explanations of the efficacy of magic, prayers, and astrology. All these activities (and prophecies) are made possible by the fact that each part of the universe affects the others and is affected by them, not by mechanical causation nor by influencing the will of deities - particularly stars - but exclusively by mutual sympathy.

I think, therefore, that those ancient sages, who sought to secure the presence of divine beings by the erection of shrines and

statues, showed insight into the nature of the All; they perceived
that, though this Soul is everywhere tractable, its presence will be
secured all the more readily when an appropriate receptacle is
elaborated, a place especially capable of receiving some portion
or phase of it, something reproducing it, or representing it and
serving like a mirror to catch an image of it (IV – 3:11).

There is no clearer an exposition of the Christian New Testament
statement concerning "men taking the heavens by violence," than
Plotinus' view of the great leap upward toward the Supreme by creative
souls through time immemorial.

## Matter

As to matter, Plotinus in the writings of this period - with less
ambiguity than in other periods - characterizes it as the result of the last
step of the emanative process, thus fully preserving the monistic
character of his system.

He faults certain schools of his day regarding their erroneous
conceptions of matter. Regarding the Epicureans, he writes:

To a certain school, body-forms exclusively are the Real Beings;
existence is limited to bodies; there is one only Matter, the stuff
underlying the primal-constituents of the Universe: existence is
nothing but this Matter: everything is some modification of this;
the elements of the Universe are simply this Matter in a certain
condition.

Plotinus attacks the "audacity" of the Epicureans "to foist Matter
upon the divine beings so that, finally, God himself becomes a mode of
Matter - and this though they make it corporeal, describing it as a body
void of quality, but a magnitude (II – 5:5)."

As for the Stoics and their idealistic philosophy, Plotinu argues
that they make "incorporeal: among these, not all hold the theory of one
only Matter; some of them while they maintain the one Matter, in
which the first school believes, the foundation of bodily forms, admit
another, existing in the divine-sphere, the base of the Ideas there and of
the unembodied Beings (II – 5:5)."

Empedokles in identifying his "elements" with Matter is refuted
by their decay. Anaxagoras, in identifying his "primal-combination"

with Matter - to which he allots no mere aptness to any and every nature or quality but the effective possession of all - withdraws in this way the very *Nous* he had introduced; for this Mind is not to him the bestower of shape, of Forming Idea; and it is co-equal with Matter, not its prior. But this simultaneous existence is impossible: for if the combination derives Being by participation, Being is the prior; if both are Authentic Existents, then an additional Principle, a third, is imperative [a ground of unification]. But pantheistic tendencies must be rejected.

That all is in all is impossible, according to Plotinus. The baser things cannot be equal to "the infinite" and those schools that attempt this union need to carefully define their terms. "If this "infinite" means "of endless extension" there is no infinite among beings; there is neither an infinity-in-itself [Infinity Abstract] nor an infinity as an attribute to some body," he writes. In the first case every part of that infinity would be infinite and in the second an object in which the infinity was present as an attribute could not be infinite apart from that attribute, could not be Matter.

Atoms again cannot meet the need of a base. There are no atoms; all body is divisible endlessly: besides neither the continuity nor the ductility of corporeal things is explicable apart from Mind, or apart from the Soul which cannot be made up of atoms; and, again, out of atoms creation could produce nothing but atoms: a creative power could produce nothing from a material devoid of continuity. Any number of reasons might be brought, and have been brought, against this hypothesis and it need detain us no longer.

What, then, is this Kind, this Matter, described as one stuff, continuous and without quality? Clearly since it is without quality it is incorporeal; bodiliness would be quality. It must be the basic stuff of all the entities of the sense-world and not merely base to some while being to others achieved form.

Take for example, the clay of a potter. Although it is matter that the potter uses to create there is much more to clay than just its sensory qualities. Here we see the integration of the idealist concept that the mind somehow creates the idea and existence of this clay above and beyond its simple properties. Plotinus wayst that "we must therefore refuse to it all that we find in things of sense- not merely such attributes as color, heat or cold, but weight or weightlessness, thickness or thinness, shape and therefore magnitude; though notice that to be present within magnitude and shape is very different from possessing these qualities."

It cannot be a compound, it must be a simplex, one distinct thing in its nature; only so can it be void of all quality. The Principle which gives it form gives this as something alien: so with magnitude and all really-existent things bestowed upon it. If, for example, it possessed a magnitude of its own, the Principle giving it form would be at the mercy of that magnitude and must produce not at will, but only within the limit of the Matter's capacity: to imagine that Will keeping step with its material is fantastic.

> The Matter must be of later origin than the forming-power, and therefore must be at its disposition throughout, ready to become anything, ready therefore to any bulk; besides, if it possessed magnitude, it would necessarily possess shape also: it would be doubly inductile.

> Matter, for Plotinus, is Potentiality. It is not Actualization, for if it were it would not be disassociated from Authentic Being. It is a muddled way to put it, but Plotinus writes that "the thing having its Being in Non-Beingness: for, note, in the case of things whose Being is a falsity, to take away the falsity is to take away what Being they have." If we introduce actualization into things whose Being and Essence is Potentiality the foundation of their very nature is destroyed.

---

*Endnotes*

[1] C.S. Lewis, *Mere Christianity* (Huntington, N.Y.: J.M. Fontana Publishing, 1955), pp. 135-38.
[2] Swami Vivekananda, *The Works of Swami Vivekananda*, vol. 7, pp. 128-29.

# 10
# Mystic and Metaphysician

Plotinus' reputation as a mystical writer with a somewhat awkward style has resulted in his often being misunderstood, even neglected, by most traditions which embrace the classical tradition of ancient philosophy and even more so, perhaps, by those traditions which base their religious and philosophic thought on historical drama; Plotinus' idealistic world is spiritual through and through and does not entertain thoughts of an historical reality.

Plotinus' philosophy is based largely on the thinking of Plato, and Plato's mystical philosophy, for Plotinus, is an inspired authority. Of course, the student managed in many ways to carve out a great space of originality in his own thinking but the master's influence remained foundational.

The writing of Plotinus, its mystical overtones rich with the vocabulary and imagery of spiritual reality, although it has attracted much critical comment over the centuries, nonetheless present him as a spiritual guide with profound insight into a universe "bound with gold chains about the feet of God."

Augustine, Dante, Schiller, and Wordsworth, to name but a few, are examples of the theologians, philosophers, poets, and musicians who in some form or fashion embraced Plotinus' mystical philosophy down through the portals of time.

## Augustine

The Christian theology of late antiquity was strongly influenced by Plotinus' strong emphasis the Divine's transcendent nature, the struggle for man to overcome the Soul's trappings, and on the return of the Soul to unity with the Divine but at the same time many Christian writers subordinate Plotinus' influence in their own writings or either rejected him outright because his doctrines were in opposition to such concepts as the Trinity and the incarnation, crucifixion, and resurrection of Christ.

The first great Christian philosopher, Augustine (354-430), borrowed Plotinus' ideas for large portions of his writings on the doctrine of the Soul, Providence, the Transcendence of God, on evil as the negation of good, on freedom, and on time and eternity.

He quotes Plotinus by name at least five times in his works and shows his acquaintance with *The Enneads* quite clearly. In his City of God, Augustine writes:

> That great Plotinus, therefore, says that the individual Soul, in which class he comprehends the souls of the blessed immortals who inhabit heaven, has no nature superior to it save God, the Creator of the world and the Soul itself, and that these blessed spirits derive their blessed life, and the light of truth, from the same source as ourselves (X, 2).

And, in another passage:

> The Platonist Plotinus discourses on Providence and from the beauty of the flower and foliage proves that from the supreme God, whose beauty is unseen and ineffable, Providence reaches down even to these earthly things below...(X, 14).

And, again:

> For that vision of God is the beauty of a vision so great that Plotinus does not hesitate to say that he who enjoys all other blessings in abundance, and has not this, is supremely miserable (X, 16).

## Dante, Schiller, and Spenser

The great Italian poet, Alighieri Dante (1265-1321), in his *Paradiso* puts forth a mystic vision which parallels that of Plotinus in his writings. A comparison of a portion of one of *Paridiso's* Cantos to Plotinus' Treatises reveals this. From Canto I:

> The glory of Him who moveth all things doth penetrate the entire universe, shining forth more here and less there. In that heaven

which most receiveth of His light was I, and there beheld things which none descending Thence hath either knowledge or power to relate; because when approaching its desire the mind becomes so rapt that memory cannot return upon its track (1-9).

And, from *Ennead VI*:

He is, Himself, that outer, He the encompassment and measure of all things; or rather He is within, at the innermost depths; the outer, circling round Him, so to speak, and wholly dependent upon Him, is Reason-Principle and Intellectual-Principle (8:18).

The German playwright, poet, historian, and philosopher most certainly was influenced by Plotinus. From his *Theosophie des Julius*:

Love is only the reflection of this one power, the attraction toward the excellent. When I love, I become richer to the extent of that which I love. Forgiveness is the recovering of an alienated property, hatred a prolonged suicide, egoism the utmost indigence of a created being. The man who has brought it to such a pitch that he gathers up all the beauty, power, excellence in nature, and of this multiplicity finds the unity, has already come very much nearer God. All creation flows into his personality. If every man loved all men, each would possess the All.

The Florentine philosopher Marsilio Ficino (1433-1499) translated Plotinus into Latin wrote four *Hymnes* which are a striking example of the Plotinian influence. From his *Hymne in Honour of Beautie*:

And then conforming it into the light,
Which in it self it hath remaining still
Of that first Sun, yet sparkling in his sight,
Thereof he fashions in his higher skill,
An heavenly beauty to his fancies will,
And it embracing in his mind enter,
The mirror of his own thought doth admire.

## Mystical Experience

The examples above serve to both show the influence of Plotinus on others and reveal how his mystical philosophy has been appropriated. The common theme emerging from these comparisons is the radical pursuit of union with the One. Plotinus, and the writers who further him in their appropriation, embrace an ascetic and otherworldly attitude. In order to transcend this life of struggle, the material world must be abandoned, and there must be a withdrawal into true unity with some sort of higher power.

Plotinus, unlike Plato, adopts a much more thorough attempt at mystical experience in this attempt to abandon things material. Plato was concerned with making this present life better which is readily shown in *The Republic's* political analysis of society and the individual in society. This "ethics of escape" as it has been called, in contrast to Plato, is anti-political – Plotinus has often been referred to as 'Plato without politics.'

The writings of Plotinus were originally designed to be read by an audience who, in response to the all-encompassing philosophies of Plato, Aristotle, Epicurus and others, were in search of this "ethics of escape," a way out of the rational and into the freedom only a transcendent loophole in the fabric of space and time might provide. It is striking to consider that the first sentence of this paragraph could easily read, "The writings of the postmodern individual are originally designed...," and that all which follows this sentence would be appropriate for this generation of thinkers.

But this "ethics of escape" Plotinus creates in his writings is clearly a means to an end:

> If the mind reels before something thus alien to all we know, we must take our stand on the things of this realm and strive thence to see...God – we read – is outside of none, present unperceived to all; we break away from Him, or rather from ourselves; what we turn from we cannot reach; astray ourselves, we cannot go in search of another; a child distraught will not recognize its father; to find ourselves is to know our source (VI – 9:7).

If Plotinus' unity with the One (the Good) is possible, the conclusion that such a union would lead a person to a new understanding of what it means to experience this unity would seem to follow. Furthermore, such a realization of personal unity and self-affirmation could lead the individual out into society in order to communicate these revelations. In the final analysis, it is clear that there is a movement from an ethics of escape to an ethics of compassion in the writings of Plotinus.

## Plotinus in Western Thought

Plotinus' ideas have found their way in to a variety of philosophical and theological venues throughout history. In his *Plotinus: An Introduction*, Dominic O'Meara argues that Plotinus' ideas might also lead society into tomorrow, too.

> In a curious way some of what Plotinus says points to the future. His metaphysics of the world - soul organizing the world – seems, on the face of it, irremediably outdated. Yet our impact on the world is now such that we are making ourselves into the organizers of nature. We are becoming Plotinian souls: we can manage things with wisdom or allow ourselves to be driven by unlimited, chaotic, and self-destructive desire (118).

Plotinus does not hold to the humanist notion that the wisdom required to manage our present world comes from within our own minds, however. He would hold that such a body of knowledge must emanate from the Divine *Nous* itself, is there for the individual and, respectfully, society, to take advantage of, but it must be strived for, sacrificed for, and abandoned to.

The challenge for the 21st century reader of Plotinus' mystical philosophy is probably best stated by Plotinus himself:

> I will leave it to yourselves to read the books and examine the rest of the doctrine: you will note all through how our form of philosophy inculcates simplicity of character and honest thinking in addition to all other good qualities, how it cultivates reverence and not arrogant self-assertion, how its boldness is balanced by reason, by careful proof, by cautious progression, by the utmost circumspection – and you will compare those other systems to one proceeding by this method (II – 9:14)

The question, however, of whether or not history's sum-total of human experience leaves the modern mind in disarray or leads it toward unity of thought and purpose is one that overarches the whole of history. It is not the brainchild of the postmodern or existentialist philosopher in search of meaning.

The question of whether "things fall apart" when "the centre cannot hold," a line from poet William Butler Yeats' "The Second Coming," often quoted by philosophers and writers, is the starting point for every generation in search of semblance amidst otherwise chaotic experience. The intellectual honesty and rigor of Plotinus' writing, even among the tide of critical comment, unarguably displays the very qualities he speaks of in the quote above. Combined with his passionate search for understanding, these qualities help to preserve his place in history as not only the "father of Western Mysticism," but as a metaphysician whose comprehensive view of reality is unmatched by few others.

# *The Enneads*

*Treatises* comprising *The Enneads*. Chronological ordering in brackets.

# Works Cited and Bibliography

Armstrong, A.H. *The Architecture of the Intelligible Universe in the Philosophy of Plotinus* (Amsterdam: A.M. Hakkert, 1967).

Brehier, Emile. *The Philosophy of Plotinus*, Translated by Joseph Thomas (University of Chicago Press, 1958).

*The Cambridge Companion to Plotinus.* Edited by Lloyd P. Gerson (Cambridge University Press, 1994).

*The Cambridge History of Later Greek and Early Medieval Philosophy.* Ed. A.H. Armstrong (Cambridge University Press, 1967).

*The Enneads.* Translated by Stephen MacKenna, 2d ed. rev. by B.S. Page (New York: Pantheon Books, 1957).

*The Enneads.* Translated by Stephen MacKenna, abridged by John Dillon (New York: Penguin, 1991).

*The Essential Plato.* Translated by Benjamin Jowett (New York: Quality Paperback Club, 1999).

*The Essential Plotinus.* Translated by Elmer O'Brien (New York: New American Library, 1964).

Graeser, Andreas. *Plotinus and the Stoics: A Preliminary Study* (Leiden, Brill, 1972).

Gregory, John. *The Neoplatonists* (New York: Routledge, 1991).

Inge, William Ralph. *The Philosophy of Plotinus* (New York: Greenwood Press, 1968).

O'Meara, Dominic J. *Plotinus: An Introduction to The Enneads* (Oxford: Clarendon Press, 1993).

Pistorius, Philippus. *Plotinus and Neoplatonism* (Bowes & Bowes, 1952).

Rist, John M. *Plotinus: the Road to Reality* (Cambridge University Press, 1967).